DR. SARA

FROM FIRE
TO WATER
MOVING THROUGH CHANGE

SIX ELEMENTS
FOR PERSONAL
RESILIENCY

RAGING
RIVER
PRESS

FROM FIRE TO WATER
Moving through Change—Six Elements for Personal Resiliency
By Dr. Sarah Stebbins, CPC

Published by Raging River Press, Lake Oswego, Oregon

Editor: Diana Page Jordan, www.dianapagejordan.com

Cover design: Christine Rains, www.christinerainsdesign.com

Interior design and layout: Pear Creative, www.pearcreative.ca

Indexer: Jeffrey H. Evans

Publishing company logo design: Vee Guarnaccia

Author photo credit: Joni Shimabukuro

Library of Congress Control Number: 202190093
ISBNs: 978-1-7365036-0-7 (paperback)
978-1-7365036-1-4 (Kindle)
978-1-7365036-2-1 (ePub)

DEDICATION

To the year 2020, which proved to be
the ultimate test of resiliency.

CONTENTS

ACKNOWLEDGMENTS

Writing a book is *not* for the faint of heart. There were numerous times during this book's creation that I would ask myself, "Whose idea *was* this anyway?" Often that question was followed by tears and a quick text message to my editor expressing the sentiment, "I just can't do this."

This feeling of despair was often accompanied by periods of writer's block. I didn't really understand that phrase until an author and good friend of mine gave me a coffee cup with these words: "Writer's Block is when your imaginary friends stop talking to you." I couldn't agree more!

Imaginary or real, the many friends and colleagues who rallied around me during those times convinced me that it does take a village to write a book. I would not have completed this project were it not for the significant support I received from all of them. The belief they held for this topic was, many times, stronger than mine.

To the members of my tribe: Linda, Joni, and Francine, you were unwavering in your love and support. To my Pickled Peppers Kitchen Band members: you all provided me weekly respite from the rigors of writing through our fun and, at times, raucous rehearsals—and a needed outlet through our performances. With this project behind me, I promise to practice more!

To my BFF, Lori: a hearty thank you for partnering with me on our grand Nirvana Ranch Bed and Barn tiny house venture, an experience that taught us both the value and necessity of resilience.

My spiritual community, the Portland Center for Spiritual Living was my metaphysical partner on this project. I am indebted to the many community members who encouraged me along the way. Reverend Larry: my heartfelt thanks to you for your weekly inspirational messages and support. As an author, you are uniquely positioned to understand the emotional roller coaster of this process. Your wise counsel to "just make some writing a daily habit" served me well.

There were many colleagues and dear friends from whom I derived inspiration and assistance. Marilyn, Michelle, Bob, Gary, Jean, John, Jay, Louise, Kathleen, Vee, Linda and Janine: you all made valuable contributions to this book in different ways and I am forever grateful!

My deepest thanks go to my book coach and editor Diana Page Jordan, dianapagejordan.com, who walked me back from the edge of the cliff numerous times and would not let me give up. Her direct and gentle coaching pulled me through some very challenging times.

To all the others I may have missed, my apologies. Please accept my thanks—you know who you are!

SIX ELEMENTS FOR PERSONAL RESILIENCY

From Fire to Water...

The fire speaks to me as I sit before it, mesmerized by the changes in the flickering colors of the flames. As the flames calm and disappear into the red coals peeking out from underneath the charred logs, I poke the logs with a stick. The flames roar back to life, spitting, crackling, and sending sparks into the air. Waves of heat wash over me as I marvel at the fire's humanlike characteristics: moody, mellow, joyful, angry, stubborn and, at times, out of control.

The next moment, I am straddling the bow of the raft. I feel the river's gentle undulations as it carries me in the direction it wants me to go. During this trip down the Colorado River, I am struck that a river behaves similarly to fire. I also notice that it has a tremendous ability to adapt and change without ever stopping.

I wonder, "How can I be more like a river during times of rapid change, allowing myself to flex and adjust while continuously moving forward?"

PREFACE

And I confronted this question about fire and water numerous times while writing this book.

The feelings of joy, satisfaction, and creative expression were all too often intermingled with frustration, tears and, at times, anger. My feelings of angst coupled with the nagging questions of, "Will I *ever* finish it?" or worse, "Is it *worth* finishing?" often brought me to the brink of abandoning the project.

This emotional roller coaster was my constant companion as I learned that writing is more than putting words on paper. In the end, this book exemplifies my own transformation from one who just tells stories to that of a captivating storyteller. I can sum up this personal transformative journey in one word: Resilience. It is resilience that is the focus of this book.

My fascination with resilience started long ago when I read William Bridges' book *Transitions: Making Sense of Life's Changes*. In it, he defines change as an event and transition as a three-step psychological re-orientation process we go through to accept a change. I like Bridges' perspective and suggest that transition is part of a much larger whole that is resiliency. A definition of resiliency includes "the capacity to recover quickly from difficulties; toughness." I believe that increasing one's personal resilience contributes to smoother transitions.

In working with organizational clients over the years, I have come to realize that senior leaders' desire to have their organizations be more resilient lies with the single most important resource they have: their employees. It is clear to me that organizational resilience is the composite of employee resilience.

Whether you are an organizational leader, an employee or one who struggles with change, this book is a guide to help you identify and enhance your capacity for resilience. Each chapter represents a letter in the word "change" and is thus, presented in order according to the word's spelling. That said, you are invited to read the chapter that seems most pertinent to you in that moment.

Born out of more than 25 years as a change management consultant and my own experience with life changes, this book captures the lessons I learned from my organizational clients, coaching clients, and my own life.

So, I invite you to take this journey with me to learn what I have learned about resiliency and increase *your* resilience through change.

RIDING THE
CREST OF CHANGE

9-11. The market crash of 2008. The COVID-19 pandemic throughout the world. Moments like these, we remember.

These events represent change of cataclysmic proportions. And, in between these events, other changes rock our individual lives. Events like the death of a loved one, kids going off to college, job losses, and divorces all have a profound impact on our lives.

9-11 changed forever the way we travel by air. If your child is no longer living with you, you had to adjust to the void created by his or her absence. COVID-19 redefined how and where we work, and how we related to one another.

If we step back and look at our lives through the lens of change, we will discover that the constancy of change is an ever present silent partner in our lives. It is when some big event or crisis takes place that our awareness becomes acute. We become easily overwhelmed by the change event and do not even know how to respond.

9-11 certainly was one of those seminal events. If I asked you where you were, what you were doing and how you reacted on that fateful day, I am sure you would be able to provide accurate details of place, time, and emotions.

As for me, I was camping on an island for a few days with a friend. When our trip was over and we tried to board the ferry back to the mainland, we learned that the ferry was closed due to the terrorist attacks. At first, I thought the ferry operator was joking. Then, I turned on the car radio. My friend and I sat in stunned silence as we listened to the reports coming out of New York and Washington, D.C. I remember tears welling up in my eyes as feelings of disbelief and deep sadness washed over me. At that point, all I wanted to do was get home—I didn't even want to converse with my friend. Getting back to the comfortable and safe confines of my home was all I knew to do.

The Great Recession of 2008 was another time that produced a chain reaction of changes that left people in this country emotionally reeling. The loss of employment and housing along with increased financial insecurity were factors negatively impacting mental health. Research shows that during this time, there was an increase in clinical symptoms of depression, panic, anxiety, and addictions.

I was not surprised to read that those on the lower end of the economic scale displayed more severe clinical symptoms, due, in significant part, to this country's inadequate social safety net.

In addition, I found it interesting that individuals impacted by even one of these factors continued to display these same significant clinical symptoms three years after the recession ended.[1, 2]

I believe these research findings are important as we have yet to realize the full impact of 2020's COVID-19 global pandemic. The "sheltering in place" orders effectively shuttered businesses across the United States. The economy was literally put into an "intentionally induced coma" to prevent the spread of the highly contagious virus. The result was that more than 22 million Americans filed for unemployment benefits,[3] a rising number that eventually eclipsed unemployment during the Great Recession as well as the Great Depression.

This situation placed an extreme strain on our social institutions, forcing them to evolve. I believe this pandemic vividly pointed out their deficiencies. Deficiencies that, historically, have not been effectively addressed. The pandemic also created, I believe, a crisis of consciousness that will lead to major and needed changes in our healthcare system and in government itself.

On a more personal level, with the stay-at-home order and social distancing, we learned how to work from home and new ways of relating to one another. We quickly discovered how important habits and structure are to our feeling in control and being productive.

I heard from one coaching client that the first week both he and his wife were home with their children was total chaos. Until parental roles got redefined, home office spaces were organized, and the online school to continue his children's education was launched, there was, in his words, "no way to make sense of what was happening because it happened so quickly."

How we reacted to this crisis as a country revealed amazing stories of heroism and ingenuity. With a critical shortage of skilled workers and supplies, health care workers came out of retirement to go back to work. Individuals sat at their sewing machines and made needed cloth masks for the hospitals. Thousands responded to the stay-at-home order, recognizing that doing so would shorten the length of the pandemic.

I wish I could say that the positive reactions and subsequent actions were universal. That was not the case. Other countries took action in ways we, here in the United States, could have emulated and did not.

Previously learning from the serious SARS outbreak, Taiwan rapidly responded to COVID and kept the death count to less than 400.[4] By contrast, our federal government, ignoring the signs months before the pandemic hit our shores, drove a conflicting and unpredictable national response. The information put out by our national leaders directly contradicted what individual states were experiencing with the pandemic. The resulting friction between federal and state governments evolved into genuine confusion about the role of government during times of crisis. The lack of leadership and subsequent confusion led to a grim death toll in excess of 100,000 in just four months.

The pandemic left in its wake many unanswered questions about the future: What *is* the role of government? How will work itself look? What new innovations and industries will emerge? Having become practiced at self-isolation and social distancing, how will we relate to and treat each other moving forward?

How Your Body Reacts to Change

The ultimate question, however, is how can we become more resilient during these times of rapid, unpredictable and often earthshaking change? The complexity of this question lies in an understanding I have about us humans.

I am amazed to find that as evolved and intelligent as our species is, our emotional evolution is quite primordial by comparison—and for good reason. Our brains have a strong protective, almond shaped device called the amygdala that shelters us when we sense danger or feel threatened. We do not have to consciously activate it as it is an automatic response that overrides the rational brain and prepares us to defend ourselves.[5, 6]

The phrase fight-or-flight aptly describes the amygdala in action. We certainly would not survive without this important part of the brain. Perhaps you have experienced the deer in headlights feeling? That moment of being frozen in place? That is the amygdala in action.

When the amygdala is activated, a series of physiological and emotional responses are mobilized. We may experience damp hands, shallow and rapid breathing, and an increased heart rate. The amygdala then dominates our rational thinking. Diane Musho Hamilton, author of *Everything is Workable* points out "complex decision making disappears…our attention narrows, and we find ourselves trapped in the one perspective that makes us feel the safest: I'm right and you're wrong."

Fear Can Mess Up Your Mind

Amygdala activation can produce visible behaviors like anger, defensiveness, resistance, and the less visible catastrophic thinking. Both the internal and external amygdala responses can render us momentarily incapable of demonstrating reason and logic. In his 1995 pioneering book, *Emotional Intelligence*, Daniel Goleman defines this physical and emotional response as the "amygdala hijack" or what is commonly called an "emotional trigger."

Goleman's research provides a good framework when trying to understand how each of us reacts to change. The fear of and subsequent resistance to change I observe in clients and, at times in myself, is a clear demonstration of "amygdala hijacking" at work. So important is this concept to developing personal resilience that I do a deeper exploration of this topic in Chapter Four: Acceptance.

I do find irony in the tension that is created between human evolution and the brain's innate protective device. Clearly, none of us would be where we are today if we did not evolve and change as organisms. Part of this dynamic is that of aging. And yet, our emotional response to how we age is often met with fear and resistance. This lack of acceptance and fear driven by our inability to control our aging process does, I believe, show up in our reaction to events and situations outside of ourselves.

Change is an inevitable, constant part of life and is sometimes mysterious. Even when there is no change, there is change. Let me explain.

I worked inside an organization where the employees were getting ready to vote on whether to unionize. The "no" votes prevailed, and a manager said to me in a celebratory spirit, "Great! Now we can get back to the way things used to be!"

The manager had not realized that the "no" vote had created a new normal. All the issues prompting the employees to organize had to be addressed. Not doing so would result in future organizing efforts. Even though the union vote failed, things had changed.

A considerable portion of my change management work is helping client organizations develop strategies for overcoming employee resistance to change. With years of consulting experience doing this work, I conclude that in our efforts to resolve the fears we have about change we almost always look *externally* for resolution. We search for something magical that will help us maintain our mental, emotional, and physical well-being.

I am reminded of a story that a good friend told me about Mullah Nasruddin from ancient Persia. It seems to capture the irony of our looking beyond ourselves for answers. The story goes something like this.

One day, people saw Mullah Nasruddin out in the street searching frantically for something. Inquisitive, the people asked, "What are you searching for, Mullah?"

"I've lost my key," replied Mullah.

Wanting to help, the people joined him in the search for his key. After a while, someone asked Mullah where he had lost his key. The exact location would help narrow their search.

"I lost the key in the house," replied Mullah matter-of-factly.

"Then why are you searching for it in the street?" the people inquired, asking the obvious.

"Because there is more light out here," Mullah responded.

Most of us look for whatever we desire outside of ourselves when, in reality, the answer is within us. And so it is with resilience. The key to resilience dwells within us. We do have the internal resources available to help us. We just need to rediscover them.

It is clear to me that with the turbulent times in which we live, change, with its ability to trigger the amygdala, is no longer a silent partner in our lives. It is alive, well and speaking loudly to us moment to moment. Change will not go away. Overcoming the fear produced by change and its physical manifestations makes us look externally for answers when the answers really lie within us.

So how do we do it? How do we learn to partner more effectively with change? That is the purpose of this book.

In this book, you will gain important insights into how to become more resilient. It will guide you in using key qualities you already you have—and maybe did not even recognize—as the answer to riding the crest of change without going under.

Whether you are leading an organization or someone who is feeling overwhelmed by the pace of change, I believe you will find both inspiration and comfort in these pages. The stories here are derived from my professional experience and from life in general.

CHAPTER ONE SUMMARY

I believe the cataclysmic changes we are experiencing in the world right now really force us to recognize that change is the one constant in our lives. The emotional struggle many of us experience with change is driven by the amygdala in our brains. This almond shaped part of the brain does a wonderful job of protecting us from danger. However, any fear we have emerging from a change event can result in our being emotionally hijacked by the amygdala. Our ability to think rationally is impaired and we find ourselves in a fight or flight mode.

When we are emotionally highjacked, we view the world from a very right and wrong perspective. In this state, we seek comfort and look outside ourselves for it. The reality is we do not need to look beyond our inner selves to achieve the sense of control and comfort we are seeking.

Regardless of whether you are at work or at home, this book is designed to support you on your inner journey during these times of rapid change. It is a resource for you to develop your resilience more fully.

The inspiration for this book was born on a seven-day rafting journey through the Grand Canyon, one of Nature's incredible wonders. Wanting to bring closure to one of life's chapters,

I chose an experience that would help me reboot my life. I quickly discovered that navigating the change I went through was not unlike navigating the Colorado River. The river can be unpredictable and shocking. It can be placid one moment and, in an instant, indiscriminately blast you with its water-laden fury. And so, it is with any change!

I learned from observing my raft mates, that the quality of the trip experience for all of us depended upon how each of us responded to the numerous and, often abrupt, changes the river adventure tossed our way. The river was just the river. Our individual happiness depended on how we each reacted to the conditions it presented to us.

Are you ready to take this journey down the river of change with me? Let's get started!

CHAPTER TWO
C IS FOR CANDOR

The long bus ride over, we arrive at the river's edge, our inflatable "chariots" already laden with seven day's-worth of food and gear. My giddiness in that moment is fueled by magical surroundings: a crystal-clear river, slowly meandering, the lushness of the riverbank, the early morning sun painting itself as shimmering streaks on the water. I cherish this bucolic moment, wanting to fully savor it.

Looking downstream, I see the first sentinels of the towering canyon walls that will soon be our constant companions. The immediate peace and joy I feel is quickly replaced by uncertainty and curiosity, for as beautiful as these distant natural monuments are to me, they also represent unknown challenges.

*My reverie is broken by the thumping sounds of duffel bags hitting the raft decks and the occasional "S***, this water is COLD!" uttered by those wanting immediate relief from the already hot summer sun. Our rafts finally ease into the river with twenty adventurous souls on board.*

My excitement becomes tempered by our guide who, taking advantage of the river's calm, explains the risks we are taking over the next several days, whether body surfing down the Little Colorado or cliff hiking into hidden waterfalls. His communication prior to running a rapid is even less eloquent and no less candid: "Prepare for a white-knuckle ride!"

Hearing this command, we jump into action seeking out and hanging tightly onto any inanimate object in the raft. I appreciate the simplicity and candor with which the guide communicates, and I wonder why open, honest, candid communication is so difficult to practice in business and in life.

This question of candor always emerges when I hear employees express sarcasm and cynicism when they do not believe leadership is openly communicating with them. Their frustration often evolves into anger, deep-seated resentment, and apathy. The stress this condition can cause makes me reflect on a comment made by "The Perfect Storm" actress Karen Allen who said, "Sometimes I think candor is the only kindness."

Defined as being open, honest, and forthright, candor is, in my opinion, an *ideal* towards which to strive. I say this because clear, effective communication seems to be leadership's ongoing growing edge, especially during times of rapid change.

I frequently observe how the quality of an organization's information, conveyed to employees through formal communication channels, decreases during times of change. As a result, traditional channels like, newsletters, all-staff meetings, and postings to company intranet sites, start losing their employee audiences.

These methods are replaced by employee-driven word-of-mouth, which takes place anywhere employees gather, whether in restrooms, break rooms, around the water cooler, or in employee-specific online chat rooms. With incomplete, infrequent and, at times, erroneous information being conveyed by leadership, these informal channels become fertile ground for rumors and unsubstantiated theories about changes that are occurring.

Open Communication Is a Casualty of Change

We know that poor communication is one of the main obstacles to effectively managing change. This obstacle is depicted by leadership's lack of organization-wide transparency and clarity of roles. The frustration caused by employees not knowing what is expected from them, while always a challenge under regular circumstances, is amplified during times of change. When the organization's senior leadership does not communicate how roles will change, mid-level managers are unable to convey critical information to those on the front line. The end result is resistance to the pending change on the part of employees and frequently, mid-level leaders.[7, 8, 9]

My own experience with this phenomenon occurred when I was working as an internal organizational development consultant for a large healthcare corporation. Not long after I was hired, the organization went through a merger resulting in the first of what would be four CEOs in approximately two years, and the first of several organizational downsizing events.

This downsizing driven by our first CEO, whom I'll call Steve, caused a great deal of angst among the employees and me. I had the parallel concerns of whether my own position was secure, while being given the responsibility of orchestrating outplacement services for those who were losing their jobs. I was committed to completing this assignment with as much candor, empathy, and compassion as I could, though clearly, it was not my most favorite task.

There was one problem. I was lacking the names of those who were being impacted. I went through the appropriate channels to obtain the names and departments of the affected employees and was either ignored or told that information was confidential, meaning, I would not have access to it. *Hmmmm, let me see. I have been asked to manage outplacement services, do not have access to the names of those who will need this assistance and oh, by the way, my name may be on the list?*

The irony of this predicament was compounded by my not knowing the parameters of my role during this time. My seeking clarity initially did not produce the desired results as I was redirected to individuals who lacked clarity themselves.

Eventually, I was given the needed list of names and I was able to follow through on my assignment. At that point, I saw my job as being as candid and kind as I could be when working with those employees who needed outplacement assistance.

Candor Inspires Trust

The impact of this situation, however, lingered after the downsizing was complete. I experienced a change in the atmosphere at work. The lightheartedness was gone. Some individuals were actively looking for other work, as they did not believe leadership when told this situation would not occur again.

There seemed to be a new level of apathy towards the organization, which had never before existed.

The critical relationship between "trust" and "candor" became very clear to me. I observed how quickly trust in the organization diminished when there was poor communication between the leaders and employees. The result was a precipitous decrease in employee commitment to the company.

This situation matched what I identified in my own doctoral research. Organizational commitment, defined as an individual's psychological attachment to an organization resulting in one's desire to achieve organizational goals, is an important contributor to an organization's overall performance.[10] It is clear to me that: candor = trust = organizational commitment = organizational performance.

If candor is a critical driver of overall organizational performance, then what drives candor inside the organization? In my opinion, this responsibility belongs, regardless of title, to *every* member of the organizational community. So, what is it that makes candor or truth-telling a challenge for us?

Danger Arises When We Can't Handle the Truth

In her TEDx talk, titled "The Case for Radical Transparency," Susan Scott, author of *Fierce Conversations*, stated that we all suffer from a form of Alethephobia. "Alethia" is ancient Greek for "truth," which is defined as "that which is true or in accordance with fact or reality." Put together, Alethephobia is defined as the innate fear of hearing the truth.

In more than twenty-five years of consulting and ten years of teaching change management to working professionals, I hear, with consistency, about the challenges they experience inside their organizations when it comes to telling and hearing the truth. These challenges are particularly acute during times of change.

It goes something like this: leaders avoid speaking their truth because they fear they will experience emotional reactions they are unable to manage, or worse, they fear potential retribution. On the other hand, employees may, on a deep level, know the truth and simply do not want to hear it, that is, if it is not heard, it doesn't exist.

This situation leads to the development of false assumptions which, when gone unchecked, lead to two different truths. Scott identifies them as "Official Truth" and "Ground Truth." When leaders are being less than candid, telling employees what they want to hear, they are delivering the "Official Truth." "Ground Truth" is what employees are actually thinking and fully experiencing on the front lines. I have observed, over time, that the gap created between these two truths seems to widen during times of change.

And so, what are the consequences for not speaking our truth as we know it to be? Inside client organizations, I have observed that leaders who are unaware of this gap between official and ground truth and are unable to close it have difficulties overcoming employee resistance to change. In addition, when employees express their ground truth perspective and are not feeling heard, their commitment to the organization diminishes over time.

Clearly, in the case of our river guide, not explaining the trip's potential dangers or omitting important safety instructions might result in one of us taking unnecessary and potentially dangerous risks.

On a personal level, our relationships can rapidly deteriorate or be redefined in unhealthy ways if we are unwilling to speak our truth. The more often we avoid having the conversations we need to have, the more we experience the steady demise of those relationships. Scott describes this as "gradually, then suddenly," with the suddenly being depicted in a variety of ways, like the ending of a friendship or a divorce.

In the same way we experience consequences when we avoid or withhold the truth, we can also experience positive unexpected consequences when we are transparent. In contrast to Steve, Bob, the last CEO I worked for at the health care corporation, clearly demonstrated what can happen when one is forthright.

In Bob's desire to develop a culture of trust and openness, he modeled behavior consistent with this desire—until he didn't. Though I did not witness the very public altercation he had with one of his senior vice presidents, I certainly heard about it, as the incident "went viral" through the organization.

As time went by, I started observing the impact his behavior had on employees. Simply put, the employees I talked to saw the CEO's action as the antithesis of the culture he was trying to create. The intensity of the perceived hypocrisy grew, and I wondered what the impact would be long term. I came into work one day and saw the announcement for an all-employee meeting to be held in the company cafeteria midday. Seeing the CEO, Bob, in front of the room as we all arrived, I sensed an air of curiosity and, perhaps, a bit of dread.

Bob started speaking with a remarkable admission. He publicly apologized for his behavior and the situation he created with his VP. In stunned silence, we listened to our leader take full responsibility for his actions. He went on to say that his behavior was not aligned at all with the authentic culture he wanted the organization to have.

As I reflect on this experience, I now realize the genius of holding this meeting midday, because following the stunned silence, people were positively buzzing about what they had witnessed as they went back to their offices. This buzzing continued throughout the day, and in the weeks and months that followed. The simple act of being candid and owning his behavior in such a public way, the CEO created in me and, I am sure in others, a deepened sense of loyalty to him and to the organization.

Candor Starts within Me

In my opinion, candor, which I define here as self-honesty, is a key piece to personal resiliency because it allows us to be honest about what we are experiencing in any given situation. This honesty can help us move through change and bring a higher degree of integrity to all our relationships. It allows us to clearly ask for what we need, and express what is—or is not—working for us. It also permits us to, as Scott says, "come out from behind ourselves into the conversation and make it real."

I believe that achieving candor is a journey that begins with each one of us, regardless of our status or title. As I have learned from my own experience, self-honesty is the starting point for candor. How often do we stop and do a thorough self-analysis? Scott calls it a "personal integrity scan." Incorporating this strategy into my daily routine is a challenge for me and yet, when I do it, I find that I stay aligned with my values. Executing the personal integrity scan also helps me consistently articulate my truth, even during challenging conversations. I realize that the ultimate payoff for pursuing candor is loyalty, and healthy relationships—whether at work or at home.

Reflecting on what the truth is for us in a given situation helps us avoid self-deception. A recent experience I had sheds light on the importance of this form of candor.

Any time I start work with an organizational client, I, through initial interviews, establish whether or not the client and I can truly work together. Developing a partnership based on mutual trust is critical to success.

I started work with a new organizational client and was enamored with the uniqueness of the organization. The large philanthropic foundation showcased a diverse executive team—all female leadership and women of color. That, and the duration of the proposed work, I found so appealing that I ignored doing a personal integrity scan. I had convinced myself, without doing this important exercise, that this client would be stimulating and exciting to assist.

As a result, I experienced discomfort in my meetings with the CEO and the leadership team. I ignored this discomfort and told myself that the communication between the CEO and me would improve. I was also convinced that I, with the colleague, who was partnering with me on this project, would be able to get the leadership team to fully embrace our proposal.

My discomfort continued to grow. I finally, rather belatedly, conducted my personal integrity scan and focused it on my relationship with this client. The question that was the most painful to answer was: What am I pretending not to know about this situation? In other words, what was behind the discomfort I was experiencing and willing to ignore?

My responses to this question revealed what I knew all along and did not acknowledge. There was a clear misalignment of values in how the organization and I believed we should work together. Because of my experience with this client up to this point, I knew there was little hope of overcoming this values gap.

Fortunately, terminating this contract was by mutual consent, which brought me a great sense of peace. Being candid with myself through conducting a personal integrity scan was crucial to making the right decision in the end.

Self-honesty is an important tool for resiliency because it can quickly provide direction for personal decision-making during change. For many of us, however, self-honesty is risky as we sometimes just want to ignore what we have contributed to a given situation.

I believe forthrightness is lacking in so many of our relationships and societal institutions that I wonder if we would actually know the truth if we heard it? Clearly, the CEO Bob won my respect because of the actions he took, as did the river guide because of his unvarnished truth-telling. These two experiences clearly demonstrated to me the importance and meaning of candor.

CHAPTER TWO SUMMARY

The disquieting news is that during times of change, our ability to be candid about what we are experiencing can become impaired. Whether we are experiencing a change event in our personal lives or at work, being unable to speak or hear the truth diminishes our capacity to move through change. A loss of candor leads to a distrust of ourselves and our relationships both personal and professional.

Our tendency is to seek the truth outside of ourselves when, in reality, candor starts within us. The "personal integrity scan" allows us to be clear about our truth in any given situation. Self-honesty is an important resilience factor. Once we are clear about what is true for us, we are able to make the appropriate decisions that help us move more easily through change.

Candor, whether with yourself or with others, does, at times, take courage. There is often a level of risk attached to speaking our truth. Courage and risk are explored in the next chapter, on Heroism!

CHAPTER THREE

H IS FOR HEROISM

At the end of an afternoon of body surfing and soaking in the bathtub-warm waters of the Little Colorado, we head back to our rafts. The hike back is precarious because we are winding our way among steep and jagged rocks, wherever we can get traction. I choose a route close to the river on a long flat shard of rock that allows me to walk almost normally. I quickly discover that my wet feet coupled with the slick rock makes this route treacherous. The potential for slipping and injuring myself is great. I slowly maneuver my way along when, from behind me, I hear a painful scream. A raft mate who is following me takes a nasty spill. She is unable to walk. We suspect a fractured ankle. There is no cell service. No 911. No trip to the emergency room. In the days that follow, I witness true heroism on the part of the individual who suffers the injury, and by those of us who participate in her care.

This athletic 40-year-old woman tolerates her pain and inconvenience with grace and patience. She is frustrated by what she can't do and is now dependent on us for assistance. To me, the accident victim is a hero as she never complains, avoids doing anything that will put us all at risk and, through her pain, works hard to maintain a cheery disposition.

Those of us participating in her care are heroes, too. Setting aside our own river experience, we tend to her most basic needs and some of us stay behind to protect her from the blistering sun and keep her company while others are hiking. From this experience, it is apparent to me that a hero is one who quickly responds rationally to an abnormal situation. To me, this means we are all heroes and are surrounded by them. And so, it is with change. We can choose to be a hero or a victim during the abnormal time any change creates.

Heroism Defined

The last sentence of this story bears some exploration as it suggests a definition of hero that runs contrary to how many of us may define or view this word. As I searched for a common definition of hero I discovered, to my surprise, that there are as many definitions as there are disciplines offering them. History views heroism as the empathic warrior. Psychology identifies hero as a leader and risk taker. And sociology views heroism as the antidote for evil.[11]

My personal understanding of a hero or heroism is derived from a more contemporary perspective. This perspective suggests that heroism is normal behavior resulting in actions that are right and just. Adding to this definition is the idea that heroism is found within all of us and is not restricted to a select few.[12] It appears that "the acts of everyday heroism can be carried out by all and are not reserved to an elite minority.... It is possible to nurture a mindset to help others in need, care for others compassionately and to develop confidence in one's own ability to take heroic action."[13]

Embracing the idea that a hero and acts of heroism reside within each of us becomes, in my opinion, particularly useful during times of change. I believe we are living in a time that demands us to discover the hero within. Doing so allows us to act more positively on behalf of ourselves and others.

The Hero Within

Discovering our inner hero becomes critical as we witness the aftermath of the COVID-19 pandemic. Our social institutions and a way of life providing comfort and predictability for most of us have been upended. The instability we feel by this upheaval leaves us looking externally for something to anchor us, and in so doing, we are drawn away from our own sense of self-sufficiency and resourcefulness, our own inner hero.

Think about it. Young people today feel disenfranchised from the American Dream that their parents achieved because of their inability to equal their economic success. Job security, defined by career longevity with one company or organization, has all but disappeared.[14] Designed to protect us, governmental and health organizations instead provided an inadequate response to the 2020 worldwide virus pandemic. This inadequate response resulted in fear of and distrust in those institutions.

I believe it is during these times of rapid and unpredictable change that we have the greatest opportunity to re-discover that hero residing in all of us. Recognizing our inner hero is made easier by identifying the traits commonly associated with a hero. Research shows that courage, conviction, determination, helpfulness, and inspiration are heroic traits.[15]

Unintended Heroes

I believe all of us are capable of and have demonstrated these traits at some point in our lives. Reflecting on both the past and present, I realize that I have been walking among and bearing witness to heroes throughout my life. Here are some examples that immediately come to mind.

The female college basketball star who, with grit and determination, led her team to both the conference and conference tournament championships while grieving the sudden and tragic loss of her mentor, a well-known and beloved men's professional basketball player.

The 20-year-old friend who overcame the major stresses of her college freshman year. She is now both thriving and striving towards her goal of obtaining a degree in Astro-Physics.

The toddler who continuously falls down while learning to walk. The surprised look on his face after the fall is replaced by a look of determination as he picks himself up to try again.

During the pandemic, I was touched to learn of the many heroic acts carried out by individuals locally and nationally. One story from Portland, Oregon stands out to me. The owner of several popular local restaurants was interviewed about his decision to close them during the health crisis.

When asked how he came to make the decision to close, he stated, "I was in one of my restaurants, and I was pleased to see that it was packed with people. Then, I went next door to the bar I owned and saw the same thing."

In that moment, he became emotional as he continued, his voice cracking, "I suddenly realized that all these people could already be infected and could be spreading the virus. I just could not accept this realization or the fact that by keeping my establishments open, I would be contributing to its spread."

The loss of revenue and sending his employees home weighed heavily on his mind and yet, in his words, "I knew I had to do the right thing." He acted heroically and on his own. I find it interesting that the next day Oregon's governor proclaimed, through executive order, that all restaurants statewide restrict food service to delivery and carry-out only. I can only assume that his selfless act led the way for others to follow suit, and ultimately contributed to the governor's decision.

Unstoppable Grandma

On a personal level, my grandmother certainly was one of the heroes in my life. This story about her is one of perseverance, courage, and an unshakable belief in what is possible.

I was frantically finishing my college senior coursework when my parents arrived from the Midwest for my graduation. Once my graduation ceremony was over, they surprised me with the news that my 83-year-old grandmother, with whom I had a very close relationship, would be flying cross country to join us. My disbelief turned to excitement. She would be with us when we made the three-hour trip to the nearby national park where I would be working for several months.

We arrived at the airport to pick up Grandma. The airport terminal was buzzing with crowds of people racing around collecting luggage and family members. Not yet spotting her mother in the crowd, my mom expressed concern, "Gee, I hope she is okay, and the flight was easy for her."

I understood her concern immediately. My grandmother had suffered a leg injury long ago resulting in extreme weakness in that leg and a very noticeable limp. She was very unsteady while walking and she refused to use a cane for support. Knowing how resistant her mother was to hear advice and receiving help, Mom was worried that she would slowly limp across the terminal, risking being knocked over by the rushing crowd.

Fortunately, I spotted Grandma in a wheelchair being pushed by an attendant. She smiled and laughed as her chair quickly made its way to where we were standing. The expression on my mother's face was one of relief. I greeted Grandma with a hug, gathered her things, reached for her arm to steady her and, to my surprise, she accepted my offer. With my help and taking slow, halting steps, Grandma led this slow-moving caravan of my parents and me across the terminal floor. One by one, we exited outside through the revolving door. And then, the unthinkable happened.

Once through the door and before I, once again, offered her my arm, my grandmother, not seeing the step directly in front of her, unfortunately, fell, landing hard on the ground. The three of us looked at her, frozen for a moment, and noticed her bad leg angled awkwardly. The reality of the situation hit us: her leg was broken.

With tears in my eyes and my heart pounding in my throat, I fell to my knees, grasped her hand and looked in her eyes. "Grandma," I sputtered, "It's going to be OK. Just be still. We are getting help."

My father left immediately to get help. My mother, in full panic control mode, started barking orders at me. Despite her knowing the importance of not moving my grandmother until help arrived, she said loudly, "Let's see if we can move her out of the way." She continued, speaking to my grandmother, "Mom, can you get up? Help her up!"

Though I knew my mother was operating from a place of panic and shock, I was not in a forgiving mood and the crowd of people surrounding us was growing. "Mom," I gruffly responded, "Moving her will only make matters worse. Why don't you just get people to back away from here?"

For an instant, her famous "Mom laser stare," as I experienced it, bored into me. Then, suddenly she redirected it to the crowd. The result was immediate. Without a word, she stared at the crowd and it quietly backed away.

What seemed like hours was, I am sure, only minutes, when the medics arrived and loaded my grandmother onto a gurney and into the ambulance. There was silence in our car as we followed the ambulance to the hospital. Once in the ER, we saw Grandma smiling and joking with the doctors. I was amazed! I know she experienced great pain and yet her buoyant spirit was alive even though she knew she would have surgery. Quick decisions were made, and before I knew it, my parents and I left for the three-hour drive to the national park.

Not long after we arrived at the park, Mom and Dad bade me farewell and immediately returned to the hospital. Uncertainty and fear welled up in me as I did not know immediately what Grandma's prognosis was.

A couple of days later, the phone rang and Dad, his voice more sullen than usual, delivered the unhappy news. "Your grandmother may never walk again." Hearing those words put me in a trance. He continued to speak with only a few of his words filtering through my shock and dismay.

Later, I learned that Grandma was flown by air ambulance back to the Midwest where my Uncle Bill, a widely respected orthopedic surgeon, practiced at the local university's hospital. She was now under his care.

My dad's message that my grandmother would never walk again covered me like a shroud. The only thing I knew to do at that point was to go for a hike. The frustration I felt over not being at my grandmother's side, along with the deep sadness in my heart, made me walk fast and furiously over the rocky, steep trail bordering a creek. At one point, the creek, swollen from spring rain and snow melt, dropped off a rocky shelf into a mini gorge. At the top of this gorge was a flat rock overhanging the rushing water below. It begged me to come and sit.

Perched on this rock with the early June sun filtering through the trees and the roaring sound of water rising underneath me, I sat alone trying to empty myself of the emotions that drove me to this spot in the first place. As I sat there questioning the fairness of life, I witnessed one of nature's miracles.

Directly across the creek from where I was sitting, I noticed a bird's nest, resting precariously in a shallow pocket of rock very close to the rushing creek's edge. There were two baby birds that appeared to have outgrown the nest, struggling to either remain in its safe confines or to fly off. The mama bird was flying in a low elliptical pattern close to the nest, crying to her babies. I could only imagine the meaning of her calls. Perhaps, "Are you crazy? Stay where you are!" or "Come on! Stretch your wings and fly!"

What made this scene so captivating for me was the rushing water of the creek. Clearly, if a baby attempted to fly, the attempt would have to be successful. There was no margin for error as the rapid water, spewing spray towards the nest, would be totally unforgiving.

I watched the drama unfold and noticed I was holding my breath as one of the birds bravely ventured forth. It attached itself to the side of the ledge with what I knew was a white-knuckle grip. Its wings flailed about as if to test its levitating ability. Right then, I felt my body making soft, gentle forward lurches as if to encourage the bird to fly! I felt the fear of this small creature as it appeared to muster up the courage to fly, only to back off at the last second. All the while, the mama bird maintained her airborne vigilance and calling. And then, the moment came.

With a surprising burst of energy, the young bird threw itself into the air, wings flapping wildly and independently of each other. It was quickly losing elevation when mama bird appeared by its side and suddenly her wings and those of her baby synchronized in flight. I watched as mama guided her chick up to a low-hanging branch. With a swoop and another cry, she came for the other chick, and the drama repeated with the same result.

Emotion overcame me as I witnessed this miracle! In that moment, I, with tears streaming down my face, experienced a deep, sudden revelation that Grandmother would indeed walk again. The courage, perseverance, and spirit of that little bird also lived in my grandmother. Months later when I returned home, my revelation was confirmed.

"Well, Mom," my uncle stated when it came time for her to return home, "I don't know how you did it, but you defied me and all the other doctors here. You are indeed walking! I do hope you will use the cane we gave you, however, to steady yourself." My grandmother's eyes showed impish delight when he said these words.

Several months later, I learned the full story of my grandmother's rehabilitation. Smiling, chuckling, and shaking his head, my uncle told me, "She was the most difficult patient I have ever had. She knew no limits and constantly challenged her care team to do more than what was recommended. We all were concerned about her safety and well-being and she just ignored us. When a physical therapy session ended, she just said, 'No, I want to keep going.' This was her behavior and attitude throughout her stay with us." I, too, chuckled because it was clear to me that the same perseverance and courage I witnessed in those little birds, dwelled deep within her.

The last time I saw Grandmother, I noticed she was still using a cane, though it was not the one her physical therapist had given her. This cane was made out of palm wood and had intricate carvings on it. When I complimented her on this wonderful piece of artwork, she exclaimed with pride, "If I'm gonna have a cane, it's gonna be one with class." Indeed, she was one of the classiest, most courageous, heroic women I have ever known!

A Hero in the Workplace

During the course of my career, I have worked with a number of people I consider heroes as well. The leader of a newly formed department called me in for assistance. Her organization had gone through some large changes in a very short period of time. Amid the larger organizational changes, she was charged with the task of creating a new division by merging two departments.

There was a lot at stake for this leader. During this time, she was expected to maintain work productivity by providing critical services to the wider organization. In addition, the process of merging these two departments into one division was viewed as a model for other potential departmental consolidations.

I was called in as this merger was occurring to help the leader get the combined 40-employee workforce to work more effectively as a group. Before our work started, the leader told me, "While I think everyone agrees that this departmental merger needs to happen, I have concerns." She went on, "Key deadline dates for some of our new processes going 'live' have been pushed back or were missed and I think employee commitment to our end goal is rapidly waning. I am really worried because our loss of productivity has wide organizational impact."

Her primary concern was for her employees. "These folks have been working long hours, some have gotten sick and missed work. I am really concerned that some of them might quit. I place a high value on this group, and really do not want to lose any of them."

In the employee meetings I facilitated, the leader saw her concerns validated. Among the comments shared were, "These deadlines are too ambitious," "The quality of our work has suffered," and "I do not feel there is real support for what we are trying to do here." Comments like these posed a dilemma for the leader. She was caught in the middle between senior leadership expectations she understood to be non-negotiable and the obvious needs of her workforce.

Demonstrating care for her employees, she solicited their input and created a new implementation schedule. She then built a solid business case for the changes she later presented to senior leadership. She knew the risk she faced when she presented her case to the leadership team.

She later spoke to me about the experience, "My proposal was not received well initially. I heard frustration and some anger about what I was asking for, and how my proposal deviated from senior leadership's original plan. While it was a long meeting, I just kept advocating for my employees and for the new plan. In the end, senior leadership gave its consent."

Courage. Perseverance. Risk-taking. This leader displayed these attributes and succeeded in the end. With this new plan in place, this leader and her employees successfully completed their department merger and were recognized throughout the organization for their outstanding work. She became a hero in the eyes of her employees and the wider organization.

CHAPTER THREE SUMMARY

These stories emphasize the point that we all have the capacity to be heroes. In contrast, by not drawing on our own courage or taking risks we can, as I have observed and experienced in myself and others, become victims of our situations. Tapping the hero within allows us to rise above challenging situations and thrive.

During these unsettling times, we can more fully develop our heroic qualities by first accepting what is happening around and to us. Though we may not like what is occurring, just accepting *what is* allows our inner hero to emerge. When this happens, we are able to take the next step forward.

Acceptance is essential for resilience and that is what we will explore in the next chapter!

CHAPTER FOUR
A IS FOR ACCEPTANCE

A sudden summer squall quickly fills the canyon. We all scramble for our rain gear except, in my bewildered state, I wonder, "Where is it? In my pack? Which duffel?"

I stop for a moment and watch while the others frantically search for their waterproof attire and I start to laugh. We are already wet from the pounding waves, and so I wonder, "What's the point?" I mean, the rain isn't any wetter than the river water, and it is warmer, so I settle back into my seat, allowing the warm rain to massage my body, and wash away the persistent dirt that has acted as my sunscreen over the preceding days.

In this moment, the resistance emerging from my need to have protection from the rain is replaced by total acceptance, resulting in a new and richer experience than I would have otherwise had. The lesson I learn is immediate. When it comes to change, acceptance is so much easier than resistance. I discovered that resistance is a natural by-product of routines and habits, that is, the way I have always done things. When that which is familiar is removed, resistance emerges. Smiling, and with a child's sense of wonder, I turn my face skyward to greet the rain.

Canadian psychotherapist Nathaniel Branden wrote, "The first step towards change is awareness and the second is acceptance." When I look back at this adventure, in addition to this lesson about acceptance, I see that the river provided me with a much broader view of change. Intimately experiencing the river's ecology, I am aware of how the water's power carves out new channels. I notice how logs and other natural debris change the river's course and, at times, the riverbed itself. The river is constantly changing and evolving.

Change is Constant

I recognize that the river is not the only thing changing and evolving. This constancy of change is found in our own lives as well, whether we are conscious of it or not. We really cannot escape it. Mayo Clinic physician Rokea El-Azhara writes, "Change is absolute so long as time does not stand still."

Stop for a moment and think about your daily routines. Things like turning off your morning alarm, brewing that first cup of coffee, taking a shower and eating breakfast are so second nature to you that you don't even view them as changes. And if you didn't do them? You would still be in bed.

Change is inevitable. We absolutely cannot escape it. As Registered Nurse Sarah Mensa-Kwao Cook puts it, whether we are "changing our minds, our clothes, or a channel on television, we know change happens." Even with your normal daily routines, it becomes clear that the mere act of physically moving through your day represents a series of changes.

You have had multiple experiences with change throughout your life. Remember when you started a new job? How about moving into a new city or living space? Taking a vacation? Or having a child? The amazing thing is that while these examples may seem like isolated events, they are changes within changes. Starting a new job is a change, and that is followed by other changes: becoming acquainted with your team members, finding your desk, locating the rest rooms and cafeteria for example. If you have a child, you certainly know all the changes that came after the birth, not the least of which was or is disruptive sleep.

As you observe these changes, you will be unable to ignore that you are constantly changing too. Human development is so closely aligned with change that these concepts are synonymous. Looking more closely at the word "development," I find that it, too, embodies the concept of change as it means evolution, progress and growth.

Inside your body, you experience development simply by being alive. On a cellular level, it is known that our cells get replaced every seven to 10 years, and those cells in critical parts of the body are replaced more rapidly than that. The reality is our bodies are in a constant state of change.[16]

With this new perspective about change, you will start seeing and deepening your appreciation for the miracle of change all around you: the blooming of a flower, the sun rising and setting, the weather changing with the seasons and the seasons themselves. I could go on.

If you can accept that change *is* life, you have the opportunity to view and experience it with a learner's mind, which will help you approach it with less fear.

Change as a Teacher

Experiencing change from this perspective allows you to become more like this depiction of a stream written by poet William Stafford: "The stream is always revising / water is always ready to learn."

I have experienced this lesson many times through my work. As a consultant, I know that learning from my client's actions is as important as being a subject matter expert.

The CEO of a manufacturing company was frustrated with how challenging it was to initiate changes inside his organization. He opined that he ran into resistance no matter what change he proposed. The changes were, he believed, necessary to remain competitive. He thought if the employees received change management skill training, they would be less resistant to what he was trying to do.

When I explored how he approached change implementation he said, "Well, I usually have an email sent to all employees announcing what is changing, why we need to make the change, and the proposed timeline for implementation." He went on to say, "I like using email for these announcements, because then no one can say that they don't know or didn't hear about it."

Once the email was sent, he told me he went about running his business as usual. That, he discovered, was difficult to do. He recounted, "Rather than running the organization, I was spending much of my time responding to employee concerns about the announced change. Of course, this meant employee productivity, in addition to mine, was suffering!"

I asked him how he viewed his leadership role in implementing large-scale change. He believed that with announcing changes and offering his employees change management training, he had done his part. In his desire for his organization to be more change resilient, he missed a crucial point. He really did not understand how *his* thinking needed to change in order to fulfill his vision.

My work quickly shifted from providing what he *wanted* to what he *needed*. We focused on his role as the leader in initiating and managing change. What he lacked was awareness and a thorough understanding of why his employees resisted his proposed changes. This awareness would require a shift in his approach to leading current and future initiatives.

When I redirected our work from the workforce to the leader, it launched the CEO and his organization on the path toward becoming more change resilient.

In our coaching sessions, I learned that he believed his use of email was the best way to communicate openly and transparently with his employees. It took him awhile to realize that his use of email for this purpose, was a way to avoid having *real* conversations with his employees. He recognized his fear of conducting "live" conversations. His main concern was not being able to manage potential negative employee reactions. In addition, he was afraid he would not be able to truthfully answer all employee questions directed to him.

It was in this moment, he discovered the true meaning of being authentic and transparent.

Susan Scott, author of *Fierce Conversations*, describes authenticity and transparency in this way: "You are required to respond to your world. And that response often requires change. We effect change by coming out from behind ourselves into our conversations, and making them real, even if it is difficult or it's not always pleasant. Authenticity is not something you have—it's something you choose."

Our work together was filled with important self-discoveries for him. Even though he was the organization's ultimate decision maker, he experienced that the more engaged he was with his employees prior to and during change implementation, the less resistance emerged from his workforce. I remember the excitement he expressed after the first few all-employee meetings he conducted.

He said to me, "I now know that communicating once about a change is not sufficient for employees to support it. I discovered that using our internal employee newsletter, holding frequent meetings, and posting updates on the company intranet are all ways I can effectively present my case for change."

He went on, "How I interact with employees is equally as important. Showing my enthusiasm for what will be happening and making sure the employees understand how they will benefit from any change I want to make, will go a long way in helping them get on board."

He had learned that making a change initiative a shared experience with his employees was critical for success.

This insight also influenced his original thinking about the training he wanted to offer his workforce. He now recognized that training needed to be more than just addressing change concepts. It needed to focus on building the skills critical for becoming an effective change leader. He wanted to cultivate in his employees the same skills he had learned.

The result of all this work was profound. Signs that his organization was becoming more change resilient were appearing when I checked in with him after some time had passed. He told me, "Yes, there are challenges, and I am feeling more confident about my ability to address them." He also acknowledged that there had been some employee attrition. He said, "I do not view this situation as a negative. Our newly hired employees are much more aligned with the company's emerging change culture; one of adaptability and resilience."

In addition, his ongoing engagement activities allowed him to experience his employees' workday realities. He valued this information as it helped him develop more realistic strategies around implementing change. This insight was important. I pointed out that he was, through his actions, closing the gap between what Susan Scott identifies as "official and ground truth." He expressed it best by saying, "I now have a much better understanding of what is really [Ground Truth] going on inside the company, rather than what I assume or want to believe [Official Truth] is happening."

The Fear Related to Change

Early in my work with the CEO, I recognized the uncertainty and fear both he and his employees were experiencing with change. This reaction is common. It stems primarily from the comfort we have with the familiarity, predictability, and stability of the status quo. Spiritual leader, Pema Chödrön, author of *The Places That Scare You*, writes that when our stability is threatened, our first reaction is fear.

When we are in this place of fear, we try to exert control over what is happening. We want to preserve our sense of stability. Chödrön explains that the harder we try to control the situation, the more pain we experience.[17] I also believe that, ultimately, we lose control of that to which we are grasping so tightly.

I remember as a child going to the swimming pool with my friends. One of our favorite activities was pushing a beach ball under the water and sitting on it. The game, of course, was to see who could sit on the ball the longest. It didn't take very long for me to fall off the ball and get a good dunking. And the ball? It didn't just rise to the surface—it exploded out of the water into the air. For me, the lesson is clear. The longer I resist a change, the more painful the unwanted experience of that change becomes for me.

Ronald Heifetz, leadership professor at the Harvard Kennedy School expands on Chödrön's observation by arguing that resistance to change stems from a fear of loss. I also find this perspective to be true.

Change and the Fear of Loss

When we are asking people to change, we need to identify the types of losses they are experiencing. Are they losing some form of personal identity because a job title has changed or been eliminated? What benefits do they now enjoy that will be going away? In addition to identity, loss of competence, security, status, and control, what other factors are contributing to change resistance?[18]

If you have children, or are close to someone who does, you have probably experienced some of these losses. You watched the children grow and venture further away from home. As a result, you may have experienced "the empty nest syndrome." In an October 2014 interview, Dr. Kyle Bradford Jones, author of *The Dangers of the Empty Nest Syndrome* described this condition. "As soon as the kids leave the house, there's a lot of grief, loneliness with the parents."

Associated with these feelings is the fear produced by loss of purpose. No longer are you taking your child to soccer games, attending concerts, providing transportation, and making costumes. Your child is no longer the center of your universe. What do you do now?[19]

In the chapter on Candor, I addressed the challenge of being transparent during times of change. This challenge can be amplified by the fear of loss. I have experienced and observed this phenomenon play out in relationships, both personal and professional. How many times have you been less than candid with someone because you were afraid of losing that relationship? I know I have!

In the work world, the fear of loss is very evident. I consulted with a health care system that was completing the conversion from paper to electronic medical records. The resistance to making this change was palpable and clearly created a strong fear of loss among employees. One employee said to me, "See this pencil? I don't want to give it up!" While I was amused by this statement, I quickly recognized she was not joking.

The pencil clearly was more than a pencil to this individual. It represented a way of work that was going away. She and others feared that the new technology replacing their familiar way of work would lead to job elimination.

This fear of job loss resulted in high resistance towards learning a new system. The skills associated with this conversion were totally new. Letting go of the old skill set and learning the new one made them feel like beginners rather than the seasoned professionals they had become over time. William Bridges, author of *Transitions: Making Sense of Life's Changes*, talks about how we undermine our own stability during times of change, that before we start something new, we have to let go of that which is familiar. We have to basically "unlearn the old way."[20]

Unlearning the old way was not the only challenge these employees faced. As experienced professionals, they had personal high expectations for performing well. They retained these same expectations as they were learning the new skill set, and this caused frustration. In addition, they had to deal with the expectations of their employer, who wanted them to achieve a high level of competency with the new system as soon as possible. Their fear of potential job loss and not meeting these high expectations far outweighed their understanding that the conversion would make their jobs easier and increase their productivity.

This point of transition between the old and the new is what Bridges calls the Neutral Zone or, as a manager said to me some time ago, "Dr. Stebbins, this is the Nuclear Zone." I chuckled when I heard his comment. I also recognized the truth in it.

Neutral Zone Dynamics

The Neutral Zone is where emotions are fluid and run high because we are being asked to let go of the old way of doing things and are unsure of how we will fit into the new. Psychologist Dr. Cynthia Scott and sociologist Dr. Dennis Jaffe, identify four categories of responses I believe are common in the Neutral Zone. They are denial, resistance, exploration, and commitment.[21] While each of us is unique in how we react within these categories, I have both observed and experienced the shock, confusion, anger, apathy, anxiety, curiosity, excitement, and resolve often associated with the Neutral Zone.

I remember how these elements and feelings played out in my own life when, in my late twenties, I lost a position nine months after moving to a city totally new to me. My initial response? "This is not happening to me!" Denial—which was later translated into anger and the desire to get back at my employer—resistance. In time, I became curious about what my future could hold for me, and I started seeing options—exploration. As I explored these options, my excitement grew. This excitement lead to my desire for a career change, resulting in my commitment to make it happen. Four months later, I started my college teaching career.

While I made moving through these elements of denial, resistance, exploration, and commitment sound easy, I definitely experienced challenges along the way. This process is fluid as I soon learned! There were days when I bounced back and forth among all four elements and sometimes the depth of feeling I experienced in, for example, resistance was so strong that I stayed there for a while, unable to move forward.

As I reflect on this time in my life, I realize that I would not be where I am today had I not had this experience. Certainly, I would not be able to frame what I learned from this abrupt change and its associated emotions in the way I have described here.

You may have experienced the emotions of the Neutral Zone without even knowing it. Think about some of the major life events that have helped shape who you are. Graduating from high school or college, you may have felt the exhilaration of accomplishment and the excitement of creating your own life. At the same time, you probably also felt some anxiety about the future and the sense of not knowing exactly how things would work out for you.

This same dynamic plays out in the workplace as well. Perhaps you were promoted into your first leadership position and found yourself both excited and scared. You probably experienced frustration, too, because you had not yet realized that your new role required skills you had not yet developed.

My health care client employees were gripped with the fear of loss and were rocked by Neutral Zone emotions. In addition, they felt isolated because they had no opportunity to express what they were feeling to each other or to the senior leadership team.

Through learning about the nature of change itself and the dynamics of the Neutral Zone, the leadership team with my guidance, made an important discovery. Before the project was implemented, they had, unbeknownst to themselves, worked through the same fear and emotions their employees were now experiencing. The leaders' realization that their employees needed to have the same opportunity was profound.

This insight shifted how the leadership team viewed the employees, and it led to a plan designed to support the workforce more effectively through the change. The new plan included actions, such as holding open, facilitated employee dialog sessions in which members of the leadership team participated, extending the implementation "go live" date, and creating clear employee "feedback loops" so that the leadership was kept current on employee concerns.

When these actions were announced, the employees, skeptical at first, felt they were being heard, started feeling less isolated, and took initial first steps toward accepting this major change from a paper to digital medical record.

Acknowledging the uncertainty of change, the common fears associated with it, and understanding the transition process associated with a change event are all important aspects of ultimately accepting change. A final element for achieving change acceptance is choosing how to respond to our emotions.

Understanding Emotional Responses

Recognizing that we have a choice in how we respond emotionally is a foundational piece of Daniel Goleman's breakthrough research on emotional intelligence or EI. A psychologist and frequent *New York Times* Science contributor, Goleman suggests that EI may be more important in predicting an individual's future success than the standard IQ, commonly known as the intelligence quotient. Goleman's thesis stems from current research on measuring intelligence.[22]

I think it is important to differentiate EI from IQ. EI refers to our ability to recognize emotions, identify the feelings of others, regulating our own emotional responses and effectively utilizing emotions in developing and maintaining relationships. By contrast, IQ focuses on our reasoning ability, perception of the world and memory. IQ plays a role in assessing one's aptitude for success. Research has demonstrated that EI is as equally, if not more, important as IQ in determining our level of happiness and achievement in life.[23]

I believe that understanding EI is fundamental to our understanding of how we respond to and accept change. Goleman identifies four categories, which he calls EI domains. They are Self-Awareness, Self-Management, Social Awareness, and Relationship Management. Within these domains, Goleman identifies competencies that are, I believe, critical to our accepting change.

Emotional Self-Awareness is, according to Goleman, "the ability to understand your own emotions and their effects on your performance." He goes on to say that when we have this self-awareness, we are aware of what we are feeling moment to moment. We also understand how these feelings dictate our actions or behavior. This level of self-awareness leads to what Goleman explains is enhanced self-control and emotional regulation. Do I act out my emotions or do I just acknowledge them? Making a choice between these two responses drives what happens next.

While emotional acting out may feel good in the moment, doing so can have unintended short-term and long-term consequences. This action can create what Susan Scott, author of *Fierce Conversations*, calls "an emotional wake" that can wash over those nearby.

You may have, unknowingly, initiated an emotional wake or been impacted by one. Have you noticed that, when you express anger or frustration, those around you sometimes become silent or even leave? They are feeling the impact of the emotional wake you created. Think about a time when someone at work acted out. Their actions may or may not have been directed at you and yet you, perhaps, experienced shock, disbelief, and unease. In that moment, you experienced the impact of their emotional wake.

In the chapter on Candor, I cited the behavior of a health care corporation CEO, Bob, who reacted angrily to something one of his vice presidents had expressed. While I was not there to witness the altercation, the emotional wake he created inside the organization was immediate. His ability to recognize what he created from his action led to his public apology to his VP and all employees. His recognition and ownership of his behavior clearly demonstrated his EI awareness and emotional adaptability.

I do believe that adaptability is the result of enhanced emotional intelligence. As a coach working with clients in career transition, I have seen that those clients who have high EI more fully embrace career change and believe maintaining career flexibility is the path to success.

EI, as a predictor of career adaptability, is supported by the research of Melinde Coetzee and Nisha Harry, two research professors at the University of South Africa, who found "the importance of developing individuals' emotional intelligence in order to strengthen their career adaptability."

Clearly, EI plays a critical role in our ability to adapt to and to accept change. Recognizing an emotion and making a choice on how to respond determines the actions that follow.

When change occurs, whether unexpected or not, two critical questions need to be answered:

- Do I react immediately?

  or

- Do I pause for a moment, recognize, and acknowledge my feelings, and then choose differently?

An example of EI dynamics takes me back to the river. Perched on the very front of the raft, I remember so well the utter shock and bewilderment I experienced when a towering wave broke over the raft's bow. It caught me by surprise and smacked me so hard that I tumbled backwards into the lap of a fellow rafter. Once I regained my composure and apologized to my raft mate, I just started to laugh at the scene I had unwittingly produced for the raft occupants. My laughter created a positive emotional wake because my laughter rippled throughout the raft. Soon everyone was laughing along with me.

Recognizing that I had a choice about how to respond to this experience, I discovered, as have numerous coaching clients of mine, that emotional self-regulation creates emotional detachment to what is happening. Thus, any actions taken, are based on the situation and not on the initial emotional response.

CHAPTER FOUR SUMMARY

We cannot ignore the fact that change has and will continue to impact our lives. Change just *is*.

The bad news is, the harder we push against change, the harder it is to move through it. The good news is, the more we understand the dynamics of the resistance we are experiencing with a change, the easier it is for us to avoid being emotionally hijacked by it.

When we understand that there are types of fear behind the resistance, we are better able to address it when it emerges. Both the sense of loss and the uncertainty about the future are significant contributors to our experiencing resistance.

This knowledge, coupled with the concepts of EI [Emotional Intelligence], increases our self-awareness of what we are feeling about the change event. Acknowledging our feelings empowers us to *choose* how we will react to what is happening in that moment. Doing so results in our avoiding an immediate and perhaps, unhealthy reaction.

Consider what Trey Anastasio, musician and founder of the rock band Phish, has to say about change. He summarizes what I have presented here very succinctly. "Things don't go on forever, and the quicker you accept that change is inevitable, the happier you're gonna be."

Our ability to accept change is supported by how well we take care of or nurture ourselves during these times of rapid change. And Nurture is what is addressed in the next chapter.

CHAPTER FIVE
N IS FOR NURTURE

My first canyon sunrise, and I sit at the river's edge to witness the magnificence of its arrival. In my stillness, I am one with the sun as it moves and changes the canyon's mood, moment by moment.

I notice the river's fullness, nourished by many sources: rain, waterfalls, streams, springs. In that moment and in that place, I, too, experience deep spiritual and emotional nourishment. I remain still and am rewarded by visits from a beaver, a colorful butterfly warming itself in the early morning sun by resting on my fleece vest, and a large dragonfly perching on my leg. So frequent are these close encounters from the Canyon's inhabitants that I am dubbed "the animal whisperer" by some of my raft mates.

The peacefulness of that setting and, more importantly, the complete peace I experience in my heart, keeps me glued to that place, until a rafting guide with his gruff voice bellows "G-O-O-O-O-O-D MORNING, GRAND CANYON!" The sound of his voice rockets across the river and ricochets off the canyon walls. In spite of this abrupt re-entry back to campsite reality, I am filled with joy, knowing that I can and will re-create a similar experience over the next several mornings.

The Decline of Happiness and Rise of Distractions

That scene stands in contrast to what we are seeing in our society today. Strikingly, in the years prior to 2020, researchers say that despite an improving economy, the prior decade has not seen a rise in happiness levels or overall well-being in this country. Our perceptions of happiness and well-being are well below what we experienced in the 1990s.[24]

Further, the research addresses the rise of addiction, in all its forms, as well as depression. Authors of the *World Happiness Report 2019*, John Helliwell, Richard Layard, and Jeffery Sachs write "This year's report provides sobering evidence of how addictions are causing considerable unhappiness and depression in the U.S." Upon reading this report, I can only conclude that our lives are terribly out of balance and that contributes to our deep unhappiness. It appears to me that our level of discontent seems to be equal to our drive for success and that we have become victims of our addiction to success.

On the river, the stillness I created and experienced gave me insight into how I can use it to bring more balance to my life here at home. I have discovered that it is not easy! I now recognize that creating stillness in our fast-paced society is *the* challenge of our time. The need to understand quietude and how to create it for ourselves is more critical now than ever. The 24/7 news cycle. E-mail. Text messages. Social media. Cellphones. Technology and our hunger for it have all created a level of distraction in our lives that seemingly leaves no space for stillness. The amount of information bombarding us disables our ability to sort the essential from the non-essential. The exhaustion this situation creates is fed by our insatiable need to know and the belief that the more we know, the smarter we are.[25] This situation has given way to what management consultant, Margaret Wheatley, author of *Leadership and the New Science*, identifies as the "FMS" Syndrome. FMS stands for the "Fear of Missing Something."

Our inability to address life's overwhelming external distractions, in addition to struggling with accepting change, are two obstacles we face in becoming more resilient.

Stress and the Struggle for Wellbeing

In the chapter on Acceptance, I indicated that the challenge we have with change is our comfort with the status quo. We enjoy the stability that comes with predictability. Spiritual leader Pema Chödrön points out in her book, *The Places that Scare You*, that this comfort with the status quo really does not serve us. She explains "that nothing is static or fixed, that all is fleeting and impermanent, is the first mark of existence...yet at the level of personal experience, we resist this basic fact...it means life does not always go our way. It means there is loss as well as gain. And we don't like that."

Learning to accept Chödrön's concept of impermanence is, I believe, at the core of our desire to create happy and fulfilling lives. I have observed in myself and others, the impact stress, associated with rapid change, has on overall physical and emotional well-being. I am not alone in recognizing this impact or its consequences.

In researching the relationship between stress and employee well-being, I came across some sobering statistics. One in four American workers is afflicted with mental health issues evolving from stress. In addition, American companies lose $150 billion annually due to mental illness, absenteeism, and addiction.[26]

The negative economic impact of untreated employee emotional distress has given rise to wellness and well-being programs designed to reduce the impact of workplace stress. A study of employee wellness programs found 90% of businesses with 50 or more employees offered programming designed to promote and improve health.[27]

While I am encouraged by this statistic, I am discouraged by the research showing low employee participation in these programs. While the number of companies offering these programs is increasing, employee participation, which is voluntary, is only about 20%.[28]

These findings suggest to me that as a society, we are just beginning to acknowledge that self-care is as important as work itself. As I study the literature on wellness, I recognize that self-care and nurturing is more than a program. It is, in my opinion, a way of being. Here is a question for you: What would your life be like if you developed nurturing as a habit like brushing your teeth?

Creating Stillness

My river experience taught me the power of nurturing through my early morning stillness time. This setting was perfect as there were no distractions. I do believe the numerous close encounter animal visits were truly the result of me, in those moments, becoming one with my surroundings.

Once I left the Grand Canyon and returned home, I realized that I did not need the Canyon to produce stillness. Stillness can occur anywhere because it is internally rather than externally created. However, knowing this point has not always translated into practice. Since the trip, that situation has changed. I now consistently create stillness time in the early morning. I am not well practiced at quieting my mind, and I find that when I can, I feel more anchored in my day.

Based on the Zen philosophy of creating fullness through emptiness, Ryan Holiday, writing in *Stillness is The Key*, explains how stillness provides us with the opportunity to "step away from the comfort of noisy distractions and stimulations." Holiday's point about noisy distractions is an important one as I hear the loud quiet in the early morning.

Right now, I am writing this passage in the silence of the early morning hours when I stop and truly listen. There is the distant dull din of the highway and the swoosh of cars going by on my street. Tree branches chatter in the wind. There is the occasional chirp of a tree frog outside my window. I chuckle, "*This* is the sound of silence?"

This point about life's noisiness is driven home to me as I recount an experience I had early in my career.

I was the program director of a large youth camp, located high in California's Sierra-Nevada mountains. The camp was indescribably beautiful, set among tall, majestic Sugar and Ponderosa Pines. The property was situated on a small lake which lent itself to canoeing and sailing activities. Because of its location and elevation, the camp's night sky produced amazing celestial shows that wowed campers and staff alike. Relishing this bucolic setting, I, with joy, muttered to myself, "And I am being *paid* to be here?"

The agency that owned the camp instituted an outreach program for city youth who had never experienced the wilderness. And, so it was, the first week camp was open, that a bus load of exuberant kids from the inner city arrived.

Their initial adjustment to camp life was a bit bumpy. One camper asked me, "How am I gonna find my way around? There are no streets or sidewalks!"

Their first meal in the dining hall was quite chaotic. I witnessed pushing and shoving to get to the food at their tables. This action was accompanied by, "Stop being a hog! There won't be enough to go around!" I suspected this behavior was a carryover from the reality of home life.

Their biggest adjustment, however, came at night. As I was making my evening rounds to make sure all were settled in for the night, I came upon a camper who, with a large flashlight, was making her way back to her unit after using the nearby latrine. She handled her light like a strobe, the light beams piercing the darkness in all directions. Getting closer to her, I heard what could only be described as sobs of fear. I approached her, with her light now firmly fixed on my eyes, blinding me. I immediately knelt down in front of her and asked if she was okay. She dropped her flashlight and, to my surprise, collapsed in my arms, clinging to me like a small animal would to its mother in the wild. Her words come haltingly in between sobs, "I didn't know it was you. How can you walk around with no light? Even with a light, I am lost!" There was no point in telling her that the blanket of stars and sliver of moon that I found so comforting and awe inspiring, completely illuminated my way.

I just held her, rocking her back and forth, apologizing for unintentionally scaring her. Slowly her body relaxed into mine, the physical tension of the fear she was experiencing dissipating. After a few wordless moments and suddenly renewing her grip on me, she looked up at me and asked, "Why is it *so quiet* here?" Coming from her city world of around-the-clock cacophonous sound, she was afraid of the complete and utter silence now surrounding her.

There is no doubt in my mind that this young girl represents many of us as we move about in our noisy world. Silence eliminates distractions and brings us back to ourselves with our thoughts and feelings taking center stage. This inward focus can be unsettling for us. Silence, created through stillness, can deepen our level of self-understanding that too often eludes us amid the noise around us. For some of us, flirting with this self-reflection can be a new and uneasy experience.

Being still allows us to be in the present moment and experience the truth of who we are. We all possess an inner voice that can only be heard through stillness. It is through stillness that we can experience breakthroughs to problems we are trying to solve.[29]

Accepting stillness as a nurturing activity provides us with an opening to learn about another form of nurturing that is equally as important. It is one that I discovered through my work with an organizational client.

Being Present

I was fortunate enough to work with a CEO named Sanjay, whose employees showed me that self-care and nurturing is a way of being in their organization. He heads a large transportation company where product loading and unloading, as well as the transportation of the product itself, carries a high risk of danger and employee injury. He shared with me that his company has achieved, and continues to maintain, the best safety record in its section of his industry.

When I asked him how this success has been achieved, he answered with one word. "Mindfulness."

Growing up in India, Sanjay learned the practice of mindfulness and integrated it into his own life and career. When I shook hands with him and engaged him in conversation, I experienced a calm, focused presence I had rarely experienced with others. I asked about his practice of mindfulness and how it applies to his company.

I learned from him that his company focuses on developing emotional intelligence—EI, the foundation of mindfulness. Increasing self-awareness, awareness of others and the impact company members can have on each other are all keys to increasing overall emotional intelligence. With increased EI, both job and organizational performance improve.[30]

Further, he told me, "Mindfulness is how we stay engaged while performing repetitive jobs." Mindfulness is the company's tool for, in his words, "fighting complacency."

Dr. Jeremy Hunter, Founder and Director of the Executive Mind Leadership Institute at the Claremont University Graduate School of Management, derived a definition of mindfulness from ancient Buddhist texts. He found that practicing Buddhists find power in being "awake, aware, mindful," declaring, "a tamed mind brings happiness."

Hunter, in his 2013 article "Why Mindfulness Matters," states that mindfulness "enhances clarity, focus, and judgment; enables more skillful decision-making; improves communication and interpersonal relationships; and fosters greater quality of life."

The burgeoning research on mindfulness legitimizes it as a critical workplace wellness strategy. Rowan University Professor of Psychology, Dr. Jeffrey Greeson, in his review of all mindfulness research completed in 2008, reveals that mindfulness is recognized by health care professionals as an appropriate workplace wellness strategy. His research concludes, "That greater mindfulness can not only reduce stress and stress-related medical symptoms but can also enhance positive emotions and quality of life."

I wondered how mindfulness, as a way of being, would show up in my change management training sessions with the transportation company. These sessions started with me being curious and ended with me being truly inspired!

My workshop was held in a large room with 10 round tables clustered close to me at the front. The room was filled with an abundance of natural light and wonderful views, as the setting for this training was in a building surrounded by a forest landscape.

The participants came in, some dressed in casual business attire, signaling their positions as administrative or executive. Others were physically sturdy, bore tattoos, had tousled hair, and were dressed in hoodies and jeans. They walked with a swagger suggesting they had just arrived from the loading dock.

As all sixty of them took their places, I was surprised at how quiet they all were. There was not the usual chaotic noise I experience at such events. Any talk was only low murmuring to a person next to them. There was no loud talking across the table or room. I also noticed that when someone was talking, they leaned into the individual with whom they were having the conversation. This action suggested attentive listening. They maintained direct eye contact with the other individual throughout the conversation. There were no interruptions.

When the session started, there was immediate attention directed towards me. All talking promptly stopped, and all eyes quickly focused on me. I did not have to make more than one attempt to gain their attention. Again, this experience was unlike any I had ever had with a group.

From that point on throughout the day, with every activity and discussion, the participants demonstrated the same high attentiveness and thoughtfulness. For example, when I posed a question for them to discuss at their tables, I noticed immediate silence in the room as they prepared their individual responses to be later shared at their tables. There was no fidgeting in their chairs, whispering to the person next to them, or gazing around the room, just complete silence and total attention to their work and to the others at their table. In addition, I noticed that no one spoke at their tables until they were sure their table members were finished and ready to share.

This behavior was prevalent throughout the day. Later, I complemented several of the employees on their attentiveness and engagement. I explained I usually find a handful of participants in my sessions who display this behavior and had never experienced it in a large group. Each person I spoke to smiled with what could only be described as pride. They all said essentially the same thing, "The reason we are as closely knit as we are and behave the way we do, is the training on mindfulness we have received over time."

A burly fellow who worked on the loading docks, claimed mindfulness training had changed his life, allowing him to be more centered and present on the job and in his life away from work. Having witnessed mindfulness in action, I quickly understood why the company had, and continued to have, a stellar safety record. Being mindful on the job helped them avoid the hazards associated with their work.

Mindfulness clearly offers benefits to anyone, whether at work or not. Greeson, again citing mindfulness research, states, "Research on mindfulness supports the idea that cultivating regular attention, awareness and acceptance... is associated with lower levels of psychological distress, including less anxiety, depression, anger and worry."

It is apparent to me that mindfulness, as a self-nurturing strategy, if practiced by all society members, can lead to healthier, happier lives for all of us. I see this as a challenge when living in a society where success is defined by achievement through doing rather than being.

The potential long-term consequences of poor or no work-life balance is well documented. Specifically, workplace-related stress has been shown to lead to ulcers and other digestive issues, cardiac problems, and chronic pain.[31] In addition, Alan Kohll, founder and president of Total Wellness cites, "Chronic stress can also negatively impact mental health because it's linked to a higher risk of depression, anxiety and insomnia."

The conclusion I make upon reading all of this research is that a lack of work-life balance makes it impossible for us to respond to rapid change in a healthy way. Making nurturing a habit, like we do work, is a way to maintain this balance and be more change resilient.

If mindfulness and stillness can help us achieve better life balance, I believe it is worth exploring further how they are practiced. Earlier in this chapter, I cited Buddhism as the source for mindfulness. There are other spiritual practices where stillness and mindfulness flourish.

Taking Time Out and Nature

In conversations with a dear friend of mine who is Jewish, I learned that what I am calling stillness is what his faith practices as Sabbath, a full 24 hours once a week, Friday evening to Saturday evening. During this time, Jews abstain from all work-related activities. Any activity designed to produce an outcome is put on hold for that period, including meal preparation. All of that is done in advance.

Wayne Muller observes the value in his book, *Sabbath: Finding Renewal and Delight in Our Daily Lives.* Muller says, "Constantly striving, we feel exhausted and deprived in the midst of great abundance. We long for time with friends and family, we long for a moment to ourselves." Building on the idea of sabbath, he goes on to say, "We need not even schedule an entire day each week. Sabbath time can be a sabbath afternoon, sabbath hour or sabbath walk."[32]

Muller's point is clear. We need to create the opportunity to escape the busy-ness in our lives, if only for a short time.

In my own way, I am learning to practice sabbath. I complement my early morning stillness time by immersing myself in nature. I feel fortunate that my neighborhood is in a residential forest. Thus, going for regular walks is becoming part of my nurturing routine. I mention the forest because of the Japanese practice of forest bathing.

Forest bathing is nothing more than just being out among the trees. Recognizing the importance of this activity, the Japanese made this practice part of a national public health program in 1982.

Writing in *Time Magazine*, Dr. Qing Li, author of *Forest Bathing: How Trees Can Help You Find Health and Happiness*, writes, "The sounds of the forest, the scent of the trees, the sunlight playing through the leaves, the fresh, clean air—these things give us a sense of comfort. They ease our stress and worry, help us to relax and to think more clearly. Being in nature can restore our mood, give us back our energy and vitality, refresh and rejuvenate us."[33]

Though the Grand Canyon is not a forest, you could say I was bathed for seven days in the magnificence of this natural wonder. During this time, I observed how easy it is to continue a state of doing rather than being.

Doing vs Being

Watching my raft mates fumbling with their cell phones, talking about the lives they physically left behind, I wondered how much of their current experience on the river they were going to miss. As the days went by, I experienced a shift, and my raft mates did as well, as we released the doing part of our lives and more fully embraced the being. Concurrently, we bonded more deeply with the Canyon and with each other.

The stillness and mindfulness resulting in a being rather than a doing mindset does not come easily for me nor for others I know. Yet, most of us have experienced it in some form when removed from our regular routines. The challenge becomes one of trying to integrate stillness and mindfulness into our regular daily lives.

Creating Sabbath, which literally means "to rest from labor," is one way to cultivate stillness and mindfulness. While this activity is derived from, and practiced in, many religions, it can be effectively followed regardless of religious or spiritual preference, if any.

Wondering what I would find when I searched online for ways to practice Sabbath, I was surprised to find innumerable listings for both secular and non-secular approaches to this practice. Among some of the more interesting titles were "Shabbat, Millennial Style," "Why I started Practicing Sabbath" and

"Why the Sabbath: The Key to Our Survival." We should note that the spelling of the word, both with and without the "h" is correct. Both forms are pronounced "Shabbat." These titles, and others I discovered, suggest that Sabbath is a popular topic, driven, I am sure, by our wanting to look for ways to bring more stillness and mindfulness into our lives.

The many suggestions I found for practicing Sabbath will, I believe, when pursued with intention, start creating the stillness and mindfulness we are seeking. One suggestion is for us to start living our lives unplugged for a period of time.

Just how easy is it for us to disconnect from technology? I was amused by a social media posting I saw recently. There was a picture of a cabin, off the grid in the woods. The caption was a question: "For $10,000, would you be able to live in this cabin without your technology devices for a year?" In more realistic terms, I choose to rephrase this question: "How frequently and how long am I willing to be unplugged from my technology?" This question is followed by another, "What can I do during this time that will allow me to connect with myself through stillness and mindfulness?"

For my trip down the Colorado River, I left my cell phone in my hotel room. I had purchased a camera specifically for this trip so that I could leave my phone behind. The initial two-to-three days, I was amazed at how frequently I would reach for my phone, and I watched others do the same. Given that there is no cell or internet service at the bottom of the Grand Canyon, I was surprised at how frustrated some of my raft mates were when they couldn't immediately post a picture they had taken to their social media accounts. I wondered, was taking the picture an intentional act of truly capturing the beauty of the Canyon? Or was it just a way of saying, "Here I am?"

I suspect for many of us, giving up our devices for even a short period of time would be a healthy place to start. I have started experimenting with this idea by first, leaving my phone behind when I go for my morning workout. I don't need it and usually end up leaving it locked up in my car. Without the phone's presence, I notice the silly little habit I have when I do have it.

While my state has a strict law prohibiting handheld use of the phone when driving, I am now aware of how often I would sneak a peek at it when at a stoplight. I was not even conscious of this habit until my phone was unavailable to me. Now, without my phone as a distraction and driving with the radio off, I am, even though I am driving, creating space for stillness.

Earlier in this chapter I cited Muller who suggested Sabbath can be created in whatever way or time frame desired. The amount of time is not as important as how that time is spent. Perhaps your Sabbath is taking 20 minutes out of your day in five-minute increments to just close your eyes and breathe deeply. Maybe it's never getting out of your pajamas, curling up on the couch with a cup of tea, and reading that overdue library book that is sitting by your bedside unopened.

If there was a silver lining to the COVID-19 pandemic, it was that it forced us to stay home and spend more time with ourselves. I found this time to be particularly nurturing as it allowed me to truly be in the moment. I kept asking myself the question, "What will bring me happiness right here, right now?" Asking this question throughout the day allowed my creative spirit to flourish, and it gifted me with an extended period of inner peace. For me, the social isolation was an opportunity to experience, for an extended time, the practice of mindfulness. This practice has now become a habit, one that I covet. Others I spoke to about this time had very different experiences.

For many of them, staying home when not working remotely, was filled with home projects. They were ecstatic to finally have the time to complete the to-do list. However, when their lists were complete, they expressed frustration, "Now, what will I do?"

The choice is up to us. Taking the time to create and pursue nurturing activities requires commitment. The rewards, as I have found, are significant. Deborah Day, Catholic nun and social activist says, "Nourishing yourself in a way that helps you blossom in the direction that you want to go is attainable and you are worth the effort."

CHAPTER FIVE SUMMARY

The rapid pace of life and our attempt to keep up with it has left us exhausted mentally, spiritually, and emotionally. I do believe that this condition leaves us less able to respond to change in a more positive and proactive way.

Getting caught up in the *doing* of life, whether at work or home, does translate into our being out of touch with ourselves. This disconnection with self can and does lead to higher instances of stress and declining emotional and physical health. I know that employers recognize this, as evidenced by the growth in wellness programs. There is, however, a troubling trend.

While employers recognize the importance and value of these programs, it doesn't seem like employees share that view. As the number of these programs has grown, employee participation has actually decreased.

And yet, when employees embrace the concept and participate, as they did in Sanjay's company, the positive results for both the company employees are apparent. The company's exceptional safety record coupled with employees feeling centered and fully present at both home and work fully endorses mindfulness as an important wellness or nurturing strategy.

Taking time to enjoy nature, creating our own personal sabbath time, and practicing mindfulness, are all restorative activities. If done on a regular basis, these activities can help ground us, regardless of the changes occurring in our lives.

Ryan Holiday in his book *Stillness is the_Key*, reveals that, "One of the simplest and most accessible entry points into stillness is gratitude."

"G" in the word C.H.A.N.G.E. stands for Gratitude, and it is the subject we will explore next.

CHAPTER SIX

G IS FOR GRATITUDE

Taken out of my normal living situation with all of its amenities,
*I feel a deepening gratitude for all I **do** have. And, with that,*
another great life lesson gained on the Colorado River! The true
power and meaning of gratitude are my constant companions on
this trip. Curled up in my sleeping bag on my comfy cot, I'm
grateful that I am not on the sandy and rocky ground. Grateful
for sleeping under the stars, even when my view is interrupted
by clouds and rain. Grateful for the tarp I throw over my cot
and anchor under its legs, keeping me dry. And, grateful for the
portable potty that eliminates my having to dig my own potty hole.

I mention these things because living in gratitude allows me the
freedom to embrace the total magic of my river experience: sleeping

under a magnificent blanket of stars, feeling the rain tapping on the tarp as it gently lulls me to sleep, and witnessing the best vistas on the river while responding to nature's call.

Poet Audre Lorde once said, "We are all more blind to what we have than what we have not." On the river, it certainly would have been easy to complain about the lack of modern amenities and completely overlook what was present that made life on the river the exciting adventure it was.

Gratitude as a Choice

The river allowed me to experience the true power of gratitude, which is defined as "the appreciation of what is valuable and meaningful to oneself; it is a general state of thankfulness and/or appreciation."[34] Being grateful for what I *did* have allowed me to more fully embrace all that this river adventure had to offer me. And I was able to do so without judgment or fear.

What would it be like if we approached change from a place of gratitude? Might we view the changing situations from a more grounded and peaceful place?

Consider a group of both day and night shift nurses who were caught up in the complete reorganization of their department. This process totally disrupted workflow and reporting structures. They expressed high anxiety about how the changes could negatively impact them and, ultimately, the patients under their care. One nurse complained, "None of us was consulted about how to make this reorganization happen, and that really makes me mad!" Others chimed in and soon the room was filled with negative chatter. I heard words like angry, frustrated, and disbelief.

As the venting started to slow, I asked them what they were grateful for in that moment. They looked puzzled. The room fell silent as they took a moment to ponder the question. One nurse, I noticed, was fidgeting in her seat and after a few moments, she stopped, the deep furrow on her brow disappeared, and her eyes lit up. She stated, "I know we were never asked for our input into this change and deep down, we all know it is really needed. Look at how hospitals in our area and across the country are struggling with cost containment. I am starting to see that this move may be leadership's way of saving our jobs. I am really grateful for that!"

Another nurse joined in, "You know, we have been complaining about some of the inefficiencies that exist in the way we provide care. With this department restructuring underway, I now realize that someone did indeed hear us— that is a good thing."

As their sharing continued, they started identifying what was *not* going to change. Among the things that would remain the same included the physical location of their unit, the staffing levels of their patient care teams, and the leadership of their unit.

The conversation that began with expressions of anger evolved into gratitude for what they had and, eventually, curiosity about the future. Once they expressed gratitude that their unit was not physically moving, they were liberated to explore how the chaos brought about by the department reorganization could, in the end, actually enhance patient care. The smiles and chatter filled the room as they started to talk about how to make the reorganization work.

This situation was an important lesson in how gratitude can provide support when moving through change. While the nurses continued to experience spells of anxiety and fear sparked by this change, they focused on what they were grateful for in those moments. Doing so helped them redirect their energies in a positive way. It is clear that "gratitude seems to directly foster social support, and to protect people from stress and depression."[35]

In his groundbreaking research on gratitude, Dr. Robert A. Emmons states, "Grateful thinking fosters the savoring of positive life experiences and situations so that people can extract the maximum possible satisfaction and enjoyment from their circumstances."[36] By focusing on what had not changed and expressing gratitude for that, the nurses moved forward by dwelling on the positive rather than the negative of their situation. In the end, they had a much deeper appreciation for each other as team members and for their team as a whole.

In addition, the inefficiencies impacting patient care were successfully resolved. One of the biggest improvements occurred during nursing shift changes. The second shift reported less time in the transition and more time with their patients. Another positive outcome was an improved line of communication between the nurses and their leadership.

Gratitude as a Strategy

In another instance, I worked in a new company that had emerged from a difficult and complex merger. The two organizations involved could not have been more different. One was established in the 1800s and had a long history of direct community service. The other one, established in the 1980s, was a holding company designed to improve cost-effectiveness among and within the organizations merging with it.

Blending the workforces from the two organizations was fraught with challenges. Among them was the creation of a new employee benefit program. The employees had participated in robust benefit programs in their previous companies. The news that there would be big changes hit them hard.

Even before the changes were announced, employees were seizing on rumors about the new program, and making assumptions about how it would impact them. Their anxiety continued to build as details like integrating sick leave in with personal time off—PTO—and paying more towards their benefits started to emerge. I heard some employees express disbelief, "What? Our sick leave is being taken away from us?" and "The percentage I pay for benefits will increase?"

When the program was finally announced, anxiety was replaced by open hostility. In one of the meetings I attended where there were thirty-five people in the room, the reactions were explosive. Profane shouting filled the room. Others were sitting back in their chairs with arms crossed, rolling their eyes. As they talked to each other, the noise level in the room increased. No attention was given to the Human Resource representative in the front of the room.

"Well, this really sucks!" one employee shouted from the back of the room.

"I just don't know how I am going to make this work!" yelled another.

Someone else chimed in, "I might as well not have any benefits at all!"

Later, through a smaller series of focus groups I facilitated, the employees had the opportunity to continue to vent their frustrations. They spoke openly, loudly, and passionately about how these changes would be impacting their families. In addition, to costing them more to keep their benefits, a reduction in certain benefits, would leave some family members with little or no access to critical treatments.

I heard their difficult stories, among them: "I have a large family and paying more for my benefits will put a strain on our family finances."

"The special medical treatment my son currently receives may not be covered by the new benefit program."

In that moment, they did not believe they had any options for alleviating their situations.

What evolved from that conversation was remarkable. The conversation shifted from frustration to gratitude. Getting them to move beyond their anger and resistance was a challenge

I did not believe could be accomplished in the sessions. As with the nurses, I explored with them what they were grateful for and what had not changed about their benefits program.

In one session, an employee who had not talked, spoke up and said, "I am just grateful that I have a job and that this job comes with a benefit package. I know several people who have no benefits—some don't even have jobs!" The room was suddenly silent, and expressions of gratitude began to pour forth.

The sudden recognition of what they *did* have rather than what they *did not* have was a transformational moment for them. Dr. Robert Emmons, Professor of Psychology at the University of California-Davis acknowledges this shift by saying "recognition is the quality that permits gratitude to be transformational. To *re*-cognize or think differently about something from the way we thought about it before."

Experiencing and witnessing the transformational power of gratitude, I make it the foundation of my work with individual coaching clients. These clients come to me for a variety of reasons and among them is job loss. Both fear and anxiety are apparent.

Among the things I hear are, "What am I going to do now—I feel absolutely lost!"

"I have been with this company for more than 20 years, and this is the way I am treated?"

"I am angry, shocked and embarrassed that I have lost my job."

They are frustrated, depressed, and stuck.

Their stories are heart-wrenching. In an initial coaching session, one client burst out, "I have one child in college with another one about to graduate from high school. What am I going to do?" While he had planned for his children's education, his plan *did not* include losing the income from his position. He had a severance package, and he was quite scared about what was going to happen after that ended.

Another client was depressed over his job loss as it meant losing essential health care benefits. "I have a special needs child and a wife with serious health issues. Not only do I fear for their wellbeing, I feel like I am failing them by not being able to provide for them. Losing my job has put us in a serious financial situation. I mean if things don't turn around quickly, we could lose our home!"

For both clients and others, I have coached, the loss of professional identity, security, status, and control was real and terrifying. So frozen were they by this fear, that moving ahead was impossible.

In my individual coaching sessions with them, they start identifying their strengths, accomplishments, and unique talents cultivated during their tenure with their former employer. Frequently, what evolves from these conversations is a deep sense of gratitude for their previous employer.

One client told me, "You know? I never really had the time to work on the business idea I have been wanting to develop.

Now I do—how cool is that?" He began to see that losing his position was an opportunity to pursue his passion of owning a business. The excitement he expressed and the lightness in his step clearly showed me that he had moved from anxiety to gratitude.

It is heartening to note that gratitude is recognized by social scientists as a critical contributor to our overall health and happiness and is a support strategy for overcoming the anxiety associated with change.

Gratitude as a Skill

In addition, Alex Wood, and his team of researchers, identifies gratitude as a legitimate intervention technique in individual and group therapy sessions stating: "gratitude naturally leads to improved social support and well-being during a life transition." In addition, the authors claim that "giving people the skills to increase their gratitude may be as beneficial as...challenging negative beliefs." [37]

These research findings are borne out in the personal story of Liz, a colleague of mine. Through her experience, I more fully understand the role gratitude plays in her healing from alcohol addiction. Highly educated, she has pursued a successful and diverse career that spans many years. She has worked in the newspaper industry, and academe. As an entrepreneur, she led a small theater company and currently has her own consulting business that she started 18 years ago.

A single parent, she worked two jobs to provide for herself and her child. She had long contemplated starting her own business and did not feel secure enough to actually pursue her dream. And then, 9/11 happened. In her words, "There are no guarantees in life so, why not just do it?"

With her work, she is committed to this philosophy: "*This* is who I am, and this is what I *want* to do." Her business has had to adapt and change over time to respond to the changing needs of her clients. That said, she has never deviated from her philosophy. In addition, she constantly asks, "How can I make this fun?" when taking on a new piece of work.

Her perspective on gratitude is a gift of her membership in Alcoholics Anonymous. Cultivating the feeling and expression of gratitude on a regular basis is an important part of the recovery process. She says, "Part of gratitude is understanding and accepting that I have no control over people, places and situations. Acceptance frees me to discover ways of appreciating others, places or situations."

What she described is AA's Serenity Prayer in action. This prayer, the heart of AA's philosophy, reads:

> God grant me the serenity
> To accept the things, I cannot change;
> Courage to change the things I can.
> And wisdom to know the difference

She explains the God element of the prayer in this way, "I am able to provide clarity and see through the chaos because

I understand there is a power greater than myself. It doesn't make any difference what it is called. It is god in the way I understand god for myself. This larger power is the basis of faith for me. And it is faith that allows me to take risks and move forward."

It is clear the role gratitude has and continues to play in Liz's life as evidenced by her successful career and thirty years of sobriety.

Liz takes her discussion of gratitude one step further as she sees a difference between gratitude and appreciation. She views gratitude as a past event or experience. Appreciation, on the other hand, represents the present moment. She goes on to give an example. "I am grateful for having lived in a town— the past, and I appreciate the city where I am living now."

She sums up how gratitude shows up in her work by stating, "Gratitude is a form of acknowledgment, and acknowledgment is the portal to feeling empowered and confident." Having partnered with her on contracts, I see how gratitude is integrated into her client work.

We were hired by a large academic department at a university to provide our professional services for about a year. The work focused on developing a more customer-focused culture and addressing the behavior changes needed for this work to be successful. Our work entailed working with individual units within the department, and with the department as a whole.

I witnessed the power of her gratitude and appreciation in our first all-department meeting. About thirty staff members came into the large room and looked at us with a great deal of curiosity. Like school children, they sat with their buddies, chatted among themselves and slouched in their chairs, suggesting that they would rather be elsewhere.

After the department head introduced us, Liz stood before the group, making eye contact with everyone in the room, and said, "Dr. Stebbins and I are grateful for this opportunity to work with you and we so appreciate how you left your busy world to be with us today." I felt a chill go down my spine when I saw the reaction in the room.

Eyes wide open with what could only be described as surprise, the employees sat up in their chairs, postures straight and appeared to visibly lean into Liz, awaiting her next words. I learned a valuable lesson that day about what can happen when gratitude becomes an action and a behavior.

When I recounted my experience to her later, Liz unexpectedly responded, "Oh?" She was as surprised by my story as I was when I witnessed it unfolding. So integrated is gratitude into her way of being that she did not even notice the change in employee behavior. I was stunned!

As we further debriefed this experience, Liz went on to say, "If I take time to express gratitude in a situation, I remove blocks from my being able to collaborate—gratitude opens doors. Gratitude gives us access to solutions for problems."

Liz builds gratitude into her sessions with the inclusion of self-reflection activities. Her doing so stems from her own gratitude practice. She believes at the heart of gratitude is personal accountability. In any given situation, she is constantly asking herself: "What am I missing in this situation? What am I not hearing? What else could I do to move this forward?" Including self-reflection in her sessions gives participants the opportunity to respond to questions like these.

She calls this a self-inventory. She says, "Self-inventory is like a business taking inventory of their stock, except it is a moral inventory of ourselves." The result of this self-inventory, she claims, is "an elevated sense of personal accountability which then becomes the foundation for gratitude."

Her continuous self-inventory activity ties in with Emmons who states, "It is relatively easy to feel grateful when good things are happening, and life is going the way we want. A much greater challenge is to be grateful when things are not going so well and are not going in the direction, we think they should."

Liz's ability to step back from a situation when things are not going well and to do a self-inventory helps her maintain optimism and gratitude in all aspects of her life.

Spiritual leader, Pema Chödrön writes, "Being satisfied and grateful for what we already have is a magical golden key to being alive in a full, unrestricted, and inspired way."

I would add that gratitude is a deep, infinite resource that is always available. It is portable. No matter where you are or what situation you are in, the well of gratitude is always full and waiting to be tapped—even in times of chaotic change. Indeed, in my opinion, the antidote for "regret-itude" is gratitude.

CHAPTER SIX SUMMARY

Regardless of the depth and breadth of changes we experience in our lives, we will always have the freedom to choose between gratitude and the discomfort we feel about those changes. Gratitude allows us to gain a different perspective about what is happening, thus, allowing us to explore different ways of moving forward. It is both a strategy and skill that when applied, strengthens our foundation for resilience.

The practice of gratitude does, in my opinion, lead to higher levels of engagement in all aspects of life and is another critical element of personal resiliency. It is Engagement that is the focus of the next chapter.

E IS FOR ENGAGEMENT

"Ok," the river guide says, "If we are going to set up camp quickly, we need your help, and this is the way it works the best." He shouts directions and immediately, we jump into action, forming an awkward human chain, passing equipment along from the rafts to the shore, and up the embankment to our campsite.

Some equipment drops along the way when movement is interrupted by some chain gang members becoming distracted. Eventually, the rafts empty, and we go about assembling our camp. When we break camp the next day, the human chain works in reverse, without a hitch.

While our ability to function in the human chain obviously improves from the first time, I notice something else that becomes a constant during the seven days we are together. Starting with the experience of the human chain and continuing with all other tasks, whether assisting with tent assembly or figuring out how to put together the sleeping cots, I notice a camaraderie among strangers that is remarkable.

One thing I notice is a willingness to offer and accept help. Through this teamwork, talents and skills of my raft mates are revealed. There is an immediate understanding of who can do what when needed. This knowledge along with the respect, trust, and care displayed for each other makes the tasks, which become routine as the trip progresses, easy and fun.

This collective understanding allows us to live in the present moment, be joyful, and commit to making our adventure a success.

Reflecting on this story, I realize that I experienced engagement in its purest form. It showed up as the passion each person had for making the trip successful. This passion was driven by the purpose and meaning my raft mates brought to each task and the entire adventure. In my opinion, passion, purpose, and meaning are the fundamental pieces of engagement, which are critical to maintain during times of rapid change.

The Buddha said, "Your work is to discover your work and then with all your heart, give yourself to it." While I think this quote captures the essence of engagement, it lacks a complete definition of what it is. So, what *is* engagement, and what is its role during times of change?

Engagement Defined

The definition of engagement is an interesting one. Webster's Dictionary offers its definition as "an agreement to be married: the act of becoming engaged or the state of being engaged to be married, a promise to meet or be present at a particular place and time." Puzzled, because this definition hardly seems sufficient to describe the experience I had on the river, I searched further and found a definition of employee engagement that more fully describes my experience.

Kevin Kruse in his book *Employee Engagement for Everyone: 4 Keys to Happiness and Fulfillment at Work* states that "employee engagement is the emotional commitment the employee has to the organization and its goals." He goes on to say that engagement does not equate itself with being happy or satisfied with work. The author argues that a person can be both happy and satisfied with work by just doing the bare minimum the job requires.[38]

Engagement, he explains, is depicted by employees who "care about their work and their company…they work on behalf of the organization's goals…they use discretionary effort…. They go the extra mile."

Have you ever initiated or pursued a task or participated in a project not required of you, because you knew it would advance the work of your team and organization? Have you ever worked hard to complete a report ahead of schedule, because you knew that getting it to your supervisor ahead of time would advance her success? Have you experienced such a strong belief in your organization's mission and future that you will do whatever you can to support the leaders who are guiding it? Or, have you pursued a group hobby with such enthusiasm and commitment that you lifted yourself and the others around you to new levels of enjoyment? If you answered "yes" to any of these questions, then you have lived Kruse's definition of engagement.

I, too, have experienced engagement and observed it in others. Take my colleague Liz as an example, who is so present for, and committed to, the participants in her training sessions that she often loses track of time and needs me to be her timekeeper. Over time, I have observed other examples of engagement:

- The nurse in the neo-natal unit whose commitment to exceptional infant care drives her desire to have the best neo-natal unit in the state.

- The manufacturing manager who improved his company's production by becoming a coach to his employees rather than being a manager. Doing so, resulted in increased engagement for both him and his employees.

- The musician, who is so committed to his craft, that daily practice becomes a task of joy and a pleasurable habit.

Engagement: A Key to Accepting Change

From these observations, and from my own experience, I know that engagement is a critical factor in achieving success, whether at home or at work. Research supports this idea by showing that there is a relationship between employee engagement and the success that the business then enjoys.[39]

I have learned from my consulting practice that an employee who does not feel a strong emotional connection to their position and organization will demonstrate strong resistance to any organizational change. Constantly challenging leadership about a given change, saying, "It will never work!" or "Here we go again!" are clear change-resistance indicators that I have witnessed.

It is because of these common reactions that I find Jim Harter's report of Gallup's 2016 research on employee engagement of great interest. Among his findings, Harter reports that 53% of those employees participating in the study are what he identifies as "not engaged." He defines these employees as those who are "generally satisfied but are not cognitively and emotionally connected to their work and workplace."[40]

It is this connection or engagement that provides the foundation for managing successful organizational change. The research on the relationship between employee engagement and change management supports this belief. Researcher Dr. C. Swarnalatha summarizes his research review on this topic by saying, "If employees are engaged during a change management initiative, they are likely to have increased buy in and better performance."[41]

I know this statement is true. All of my organizational consulting and, in recent years, change management work, has been and is focused almost exclusively on developing and increasing employee engagement. Through my work, I have proven that as employee engagement increases, resistance to a proposed change decreases. Giving voice to employee concerns about changes is an important step to increasing engagement. However, letting employees express their unhappiness and fears about change is insufficient to secure their engagement in any change initiative. There is one more critical element that ensures the emotional investment of employees.

Engagement Means Inclusion

Employee inclusion in all phases of change planning and implementation is crucial for change success. Establishing employee teams to address the change topic, maintaining clear communication channels between the teams and leadership, recognizing the work of individual team members, and publicly acknowledging team success are all elements of successful change implementation.

There is an interesting byproduct of employee engagement I have observed in my client work. Engagement is for all employees, including leadership. Surprisingly, sometimes it is leadership that experiences resistance as employee engagement increases.

With one client, I discovered that it was the CEO who resisted the increased employee engagement inside his organization

This CEO, Fred, headed a financial institution that was growing rapidly through acquisition. He wanted to build an organizational culture that was flexible and adaptable to accommodate these acquisitions and any future changes he wanted to implement. Fred was concerned about the amount of resistance associated with the continuous change he was pushing through his organization. He appointed a team that was headed by one of his senior leaders to focus on this issue. I was brought in to consult with this team.

Stories and feedback that we collected in small employee focus groups I conducted, provided the team with insight into how the workforce reacted to change. When asked how they viewed change in general, employees responded with comments like "excitement," "opportunity," and "curiosity."

However, when asked about the greatest concern they had about change, they expressed apprehension with phrases like, "loss of control," "no input," "change with no purpose," and "not part of the solution."

The final question focused on what they needed to move forward through change. Their feedback was summarized with this theme: employees wanted to be involved. Employees expressed "I need to know why we are changing," "How will the change impact me? My team?" and "I need to know what is expected of me during change."

A thorough review of all the employee feedback led the team to conclude that involving staff in every aspect of implementing change was critical for success. The team's report to Fred, the CEO, included a specific plan for boosting employee engagement during change.

In the team's presentation to Fred, I noticed how he visibly reacted to the team's findings. His eyes narrowed as he sat back in his chair. Scratching his head, he did not smile. In that moment, he realized that to achieve what he wanted, *he* would have to change his approach to leading change inside his organization.

The CEO and his leadership team would have to communicate more frequently and through a variety of communication channels. This meant Fred and his team would need to hold company-wide meetings on a regular basis, and managers would have to be more accessible to employees who needed information or had questions. Doing so would create a two-way communication and feedback system that I emphasized was an important vehicle for gaining employee support for any changes being proposed or initiated.

Fred quickly recognized that this level of involvement on the part of his leadership team would slow the implementation of any change he wished to make. Time given to employee informational meetings would have an overall impact on organizational productivity.

Unfortunately, Fred, so focused on immediate results, could not see the long-term benefits of the recommended employee engagement activities and strategies. Because he did not see the value of this work, it did not come to fruition. While it is widely accepted that engagement is necessary, this client did not view engagement as being essential for initiating and implementing change successfully.

Creating the environment for active employee engagement takes time. As Dr. C. Swarnalatha cited in his research review, it is worth the effort because "increasing employee engagement, or translating employee potential into employee performance and business success is so important to the success of change management."

I believe engagement should be so ingrained in an organization's culture that it is viewed as, one manufacturing manager told me, "Just the way we do business." He went on to say, "Our company's ability to respond to change is predicated upon employee engagement. In fact, the need for change is usually identified by our employees, because they are closest to where product production occurs. They, rather than us [leaders], are best equipped to determine what is needed to keep improving our product." Clearly, engagement is the vehicle for managing successful, continuous change.

Because engagement is so important, I spend time with my clients identifying what they are currently doing to promote it, and to explore how engagement can be improved. In fact, the content of this book is largely derived from the many client engagement conversations I have had over the years. From all of these conversations, I conclude that Candor, Heroism, Acceptance, Nurture, and Gratitude are the key elements of Engagement. I am excited to demonstrate, through a case study, how these elements work together to create engagement.

C.H.A.N.G.E. in Practice

I was fortunate enough to work for a company that, I now know, put these elements into practice when it chose to move from what I call the pyramid or top down decision-making to the pancake. I describe the pancake structure as one where decision-making, problem-solving, and organizational performance becomes the responsibility of all employees. The pancake structure is depicted by high collaboration and employee inclusion. As this pancake culture evolved, I experienced the true definition of employee engagement.

This company was the healthcare corporation that was headed by Bob, the CEO I cited in previous chapters. Bob had experience creating a highly engaged employee culture and he knew it would require a shift in how employees viewed their work, how managers supervised their employees, and how leaders guided their departments and divisions.

Bob expressed his philosophy in this way, "I know it is easy for employees to view leadership as solely responsible for making decisions and solving problems. I have learned this belief is a myth. As a leader, I know I don't have all the answers, nor do I have all the information required to make correct decisions. I also know this is true for the senior members of my leadership team. It is only when employees are involved with leadership in problem-solving and decision-making that overall organizational performance improves."

What he described was a risky undertaking for a company comprised of more than five separate organizations and hundreds of employees. It was clear to me that this endeavor was going to require time and patience. The CEO knew this to be true and said so during a company-wide kick-off meeting.

This meeting was held at a location that could accommodate the hundreds of employees who attended. The cavernous space was welcoming with its bright lights and a stage adorned with large bouquets of flowers. The company logo was displayed on freestanding banners and projected on a large screen behind the stage. While there was no music playing, the buzz and chatter of people entering created its own upbeat energy reaching its crescendo as the time neared for the meeting to start.

Bob stood at the podium flanked by the members of his senior leadership team. His first words clearly set the tone for the meeting. "I welcome you all here today, knowing full well the challenges you faced getting here. I appreciate how hard you work and how you had to put your busy work schedules on hold so you could attend this meeting. I am grateful for the commitment you all bring to your work and our organization every day." He continued, glancing back and forth between his leadership team and those of us in the audience, "Today I am announcing an initiative that will change the way we all will lead and work."

Hard to imagine a room of close to 500 people leaning forward in their seats in silence with eyes riveted on the CEO and yet, that is exactly what happened. Over the next hour and half, Bob spoke to us about what he was calling an "organizational enhancement initiative."

Through effective storytelling, he brought the initiative alive for us. Bob started by asking "How many of you have had this experience: you solve a problem or resolve an issue only to see it return?" There was momentary buzzing in the audience. With some hesitation, hands started rising into the air. He then asked a follow-up question: "What would it be like if you had the power and permission to solve these problems and resolve these issues permanently?" The audience chatter grew even louder, there was even laughter suggesting disbelief.

He indicated that we, the employees, would be empowered and trained to solve problems and make decisions independently of leadership. Doing so would eventually lead to overall improved organizational performance. Looking around at others who were sitting near me, I noticed wide eyes showing curiosity and surprise. For them and for me the takeaway was simple. Our work was just not doing our work. We would now be expected to continuously and collaboratively look for ways to improve our work.

The CEO went on to say, "These changes in the way we all lead and work will take time. What we all will be participating in is a total change in our company culture. It could take three or more years for us, as an organization, to realize the full benefits of this change. In addition, since we are going to be learning new skills and way of work, I know we will be making mistakes. As your CEO, I want you to know making mistakes is all part of learning. I both accept this truth and expect mistakes will be made!"

In the months that followed this key meeting, all employees received frequent and consistent reminders of why the organizational enhancement initiative was critical for organizational success and their role in making it so. These messages were delivered through employee newsletters, flyers placed in our pay envelopes and most importantly, through regular meetings with senior leaders, division managers and the CEO himself. Leadership visibility was a critical messaging element.

I experienced leadership visibility first-hand when I learned that Bob would be partnering with me in delivering some of the initial training courses. In one of our meetings leading up to our first training session, he told me, "I can't just talk about this culture change, I have to be visible and directly involved. If this new direction is going to be accepted, I need to roll up my sleeves and join employees in the training sessions."

And roll up his sleeves he did! In a brightly lit room with colorful training materials for each participant, instructional posters on the walls, the smell of coffee brewing in the back of the room that was accompanied by trays of fruit and muffins, he stood with me in the front of the room awaiting the arrival of the participants. Following formal introductions during which he encouraged people to, "Just call me Bob," he took off his suit jacket and rolled up his sleeves. That action, I noticed, made the audience relax in their chairs, and some of them also removed their suit jackets. Once comfortable, their eyes were riveted on him.

Watching him during the course of the day was inspiring for me. He casually leaned against the wall as I presented material, broke the audience into small working groups, and facilitated the debrief when the groups were reporting out. I even had the participants engage in a group juggling exercise.

When it was his turn to present, Bob walked by me with a smile and whispered away from the audience, "Where did you get that juggling idea? You are gonna make me a trainer, yet!" Participants asked questions of him which he answered directly, often followed by, "I will tell you what I think, but I am really more interested in what *you* think."

The quality and frequent interactions the participants had with Bob and me, his willing participation in small group discussions and hands-on activities and his giving a full day of uninterrupted time to the session, sent a powerful message to all who were present.

The mood in the room shifted from curiosity in the morning to one of excitement at day's end as evidenced by follow-up conversations I had with some participations over the next few days. Some of the comments I heard were, "What a day! I am *in!*"

"You know? I have a whole bunch of ideas of how to make things run more smoothly in my department. I have never shared them because I didn't think anyone would listen... until now."

"I had heard the CEO was going to be involved in some training sessions and I blew it off as a rumor. Wow, this guy is amazing! I can't wait to start applying some of the things I learned."

These trainings evolved over time and gave rise to employee problem-solving teams throughout the organization. My assignment was to observe team progress, refresh team training as needed and provide any necessary coaching.

While these teams certainly made mistakes along the way, I attribute their overall success to the factors described in this book: **C**andor, **H**eroism, **A**cceptance, **N**urture, **G**ratitude, and **E**ngagement.

CHAPTER SEVEN SUMMARY

In essence, engagement is the connection of head and heart, whether we are working, pursuing a hobby, or talking with a friend. Engagement is how we truly show up in any given moment. It is the basis for our success at work and in life.

Engagement also means inclusion. The more directly involved we are in implementing a change that is occurring, the more likely we are to accept it. Inclusion is key as many of the changes we experience are being done *to* us rather than being driven *by* us. If we do not feel a part of what is happening, we can experience resistance pretty quickly!

While the 'E' of Engagement is positioned at the end of the word change, engagement itself is really part of and supports the other resilience factors of Candor, Heroism, Acceptance, Nurture, and Gratitude. The story of Bob is a clear demonstration of how engagement is intertwined with the other elements.

Now that I have told the story of the six resilience elements, I am sure you are wondering "What's next?" I hope I have created enough curiosity in you for you to read on to learn what these elements actually looked like inside CEO Bob's corporation. Finally, you will gain insight into which of these resilience elements can be enhanced in your own life.

CHAPTER EIGHT

WHERE DO I GO FROM HERE?

Our last night on the river, and we sit in a circle around our campfire comprised of two lit votive candles inside a paper bag. Though the candles are small, they cast a long and shadowy light around us. There is little talk, all eyes gazing at the little "fire" while we hear the gentle sound of waves lapping the river's edge. Poems and songs written on the trip are shared along with humorous anecdotes. Mostly, this is a time for deep personal reflection.

We started this trip as strangers and are leaving as friends who shared a life-transforming experience. Now, in this moment, each of us is reliving the past several days. My raftmates talk about what they learned from the trip, and I focus on how the river's challenges became life lessons for me about adapting to change.

*I learned, and experienced, the value of **candor** or clear communication, risk-taking or **heroism**, **acceptance**, **nurturing**, and **gratitude**. All of these lessons added up to my being totally **engaged** in the Colorado River adventure.*

C.H.A.N.G.E.: How it Worked

And so, it was that the same six elements of Candor, Heroism, Acceptance, Nurture, Gratitude, and Engagement showed up in CEO Bob's initiative to change his health care corporation's culture. In his view, employees were better equipped to identify how the organization's performance could be improved. They were the ones either providing direct service or were in important support roles.

For example, he would frequently say, "Who, other than the staff, can best improve patient care? Senior leadership certainly can't. We are not in the hospital units on a daily basis experiencing the job challenges of these care givers."

Bob and all of the leaders asked, and then expected, employees to do their work while constantly seeking ways to improve it. Some of the projects employees addressed included finding ways to reduce infection rates among patients, reducing patient wait times upon admission, and reducing medical errors. This high degree of employee involvement in problem-solving translated to improved quality of service. And that represented a significant shift in how the organization operated. In the past, leadership basically told employees how to do their work without fully understanding the challenges of the work itself.

This shift from a leader-dominated to a more employee-centric organization was supported by the six powerful elements of change.

From the beginning, Bob's initiative was grounded in candor. During the kick-off meeting and following it, there was ongoing, open, and honest communication throughout the organization, within the teams, between the teams, and with leadership.

I noticed a shift in the way leadership communicated. Replacing the predominately top-down directive way of communicating was a more open, honest way that encouraged employee feedback and participation in conversations. For example, when a leader asked his team members for feedback on an issue, the team members were surprised to be asked. A moment later, when an employee asked a question of the leader, his response was, "I don't know, and I will find out and get back to you."

In that exchange, I quickly realized that this particular leader understood that building trust with this team meant being open and honest.

Heroism showed up as the teams were encouraged to take risks and learn from any mistakes they made along the way. Some of these risks involved testing potential solutions to the issues they were addressing. It also involved taking a risk by acting on their belief that leadership would, indeed, support them when they experienced failures.

A team member told me, "Our team came up with at least three options for reducing the amount of time a patient waited to be admitted to the hospital. We really didn't know which one would work the best, if at all. All of them required additional resources, and with no guarantee of success, we really didn't know if senior leadership would support us. It was a risk for our department leader to take, and he did!"

Acceptance emerged. As the initial teams started their work and achieved their goals, they were recognized throughout the organization for their accomplishments. I sensed a shift from skepticism to optimism among the employees. One employee told me, "I really thought this whole initiative was a farce. Now I see that senior leadership is serious about listening to us, and, more importantly, willing to act on our recommendations."

The work of these teams truly was the work of everyone. A department manager noted, "Loaning one of my employees to a team means the work of that team member has to be picked up by others in my department. I am proud that folks have really stepped up. I want to do whatever I can to support my shorthanded staff and the team."

Nurture and self-care were made a priority. These were not idle words as employees were encouraged to take longer breaks during the day. In addition, there were organized gatherings after work to support and promote camaraderie. The senior leadership team, led by the CEO, Bob, turned organization-wide meetings into festive affairs with barbecues and other celebrations. These kinds of activities encouraged employee self-care.

Gratitude soared. Employees and teams received continuous appreciation and acknowledgment from the moment the organizational enhancement initiative was announced. Problem-solving team recognition parties regularly occurred, and they were featured in the company's employee newsletter. Senior leaders, including Bob, also provided ongoing positive verbal feedback.

Engagement intensified. With employees expressing an eagerness to serve on problem-solving teams, leadership supporting their work, CEO Bob's clear communication about and praise for the work of the teams, I felt a renewed sense of purpose and meaning among employees. Those with whom I spoke expressed enthusiasm for serving on problem-solving teams. Others, not participating on a team, felt positive about stepping up and filling in for colleagues who were participating. While their own workloads temporarily increased, they found new meaning and purpose in their work. My conclusion was they were more engaged than ever.

This story, and the others I have shared in this book, make me wonder how these steps can be fully integrated into our lives when we are living in a state of constant, never-ending rapid change.

The rafting trip provided me with a clue, and it is one that I present in Chapter Four The underlying contributor to the quality of our experience on the trip was how each of us chose to respond to the challenges the river experiences presented to us.

This idea is explored in depth by the author of *Finding Flow*, Mihaly Csikszentmihalyi, who writes, "The actual quality of life—what we do, and how we feel about it—will be determined by the interpretation we give to chemical, biological and social processes."

Resiliency: Our Choice

In essence, how we choose to interact with our changing environment determines our level of resiliency. What we lose sight of during times of change is that we *do* have a choice in how we react to what is going on around us.

Unfortunately, not recognizing that we have a choice all too often leads us to laying blame on the change itself for our unhappiness or discomfort. Placing blame on the change or the people who created it is comfortable because it prevents us from being personally accountable for our own reactions to what is happening. Blaming does nothing to make the change easier nor does it help us feel better about it.

The hard-core truth of the matter is that becoming more change resilient requires that *we* change. I really love what Robert Quinn, author of *Deep Change: Discovering the Leader Within*, says about personal change. The essence of his thesis is that our desire to change the world is grounded in our changing ourselves. He says, "This is not just a cute abstraction; it is an elusive key to effective performance in all aspects of life."

The 2020 global pandemic, in my opinion, offered us amazing lessons in becoming more resilient. I am struck by this social media posting from a friend during the long period of social distancing. She said, "I see now how we are all much more comfortable with change, and with our personal power to change conditions." I couldn't agree more, and I wonder why we need a crisis to teach us the lessons in change resiliency. Why not start the journey towards increasing personal resiliency now?

The personal work of increasing resiliency is as continuous as change itself. I refer to this work as a journey rather than a destination. If you are wondering where to start, I offer the wisdom of C.S. Lewis who wrote, "You can't go back and change the beginning, but you can start where you are and change the ending."

Having read this book, you now sense the status of your own resiliency. Begin your journey there. When you seek inspiration, you need look no farther back than the year 2020. Historical examples of resilience abound, and, yet, we can shine the light on many inspiring examples of resilience due to radical change emerging in recent years.

Finding Inspiration in Stories of Resilience

Named *Time Magazine's* 2019 Person of the Year, teenage Swedish climate activist, Greta Thünberg personifies resilience. This young girl takes on what most consider to be the world's most urgent issue of climate change. Admired by climate scientists, heads of state, and people of all nations and generations, Thünberg delivers her message of climate degradation with poise, passion and authority. She does so regardless of how vocal her critics are, and the death threats she receives. She bounces back and carries on.

When I think of resilience, I also think of the late Supreme Court Justice Ruth Bader Ginsberg who fought her entire career for gender rights and was the legal pioneer for women's rights. A cancer survivor multiple times, she worked tirelessly for equality.

Along with these individuals, I find inspiration in the resilience of the immigrants who have arrived here and the Native Americans who continue to fight for the return of their native lands. Their journey bears a stark resemblance to that of this country's African-American community.

Consider for a moment that for 400 years this community, whose original members were stolen from their homeland to be enslaved on the plantations of wealthy colonists, suffered from oppression and violence that continues to this day.

In spite of this long history, the resilience of the Black community in striving for social justice and equality shows up in generation after generation. It is clearly demonstrated in the social justice and work of notable Black leaders, like Martin Luther King, Jr. and, most recently, the late U.S. Representative John Lewis.

The members of the African-American community have lived through the assassinations of key Black leaders and continue to feel the impact of systemic institutional discrimination. Upheld as constitutional in 1859, segregation in this country was finally overturned by the US Supreme Court in 1964. This ruling, however, did not end the institutional oppression that is still practiced. Most notably, it is found in housing and is labeled as "residential segregation."

Black families, for example, trying to purchase a home in White neighborhoods found it difficult to get financing. However, this financing issue was eliminated if they bought in exclusively Black neighborhoods. As recently as 2013, Milwaukee, Wisconsin, showed up as being the most segregated city in the country.[42]

Education, too, clearly exhibits institutional discrimination. Though school segregation legally ended in 1954, today the percentage of Black students attending integrated schools is the lowest since 1968. The 2002-2003 academic year in Chicago found 87% of public-school enrollment was Black or Hispanic. Less than 10% of the children were White.[43]

I was shocked to learn that my state of Oregon institutionalized discrimination by including a "Whites only" clause in its state constitution in 1857. This clause did not get repealed until 2003. Given that 30% of Oregon voters chose to retain it, is a clear signal that oppression is still prominent in the lives of non-White Oregonians.

The resiliency of the Black community is remarkable when you consider that five years after Oregon repealed this clause, our nation elected its first Black president.

Rapid Change and The Boiled Frog Syndrome

My own resiliency continues to be tested as I marvel at how the world has changed during the time in which I was writing this book. I first envisioned this work in 2017 as an outgrowth of my change-management experience. Since that time, our nation and the world have been gripped by rapid cataclysmic change.

We ignored the indicators of many of these changes for a long time and then, beginning in 2020, acted surprised at the speed with which they were actually evolving. I liken this situation to that of the "boiled frog syndrome." This fable states that if I were to place a frog in boiling water, it would immediately jump out. If, however, I place the frog in cool water and slowly turn up the heat, the frog will not try to escape and will eventually die. So it is with what we are now calling rapid change. The slowly turning up the heat relates to our ignoring the changes around us until a crisis hits. The lesson here is clear: change has always been and will continue to be with us. It has taken global monumental changes for us to finally wake up to it as a dynamic process rather than an isolated event.

Rapid change and our being overwhelmed by it, was defined and labeled as "future shock" by Alvin Toffler in his 1970 book by the same name. Toffler argues that we experience "too much change in too short a period of time." And futurists claim it will likely continue for the foreseeable future.[44, 45] Let me demonstrate the truth of this prediction by summarizing rapid and monumental changes, some of which I have cited in this book.

Let's start with major changes brought forth by the planet herself. The rapid warming of the earth has spawned a global climate change movement. This movement is gaining momentum in spite of those who continue to reject it as a threat. The supporting science first reported its disturbing climate change findings 30 years ago.[46]

Nature continues to rebel by unleashing the COVID-19 pandemic. It has inextricably changed the way we interact, learn, work, gather, and view our world.

In the midst of these two cataclysmic changes, social unrest and politics quickly emerged. Protests erupting after the murder of George Floyd at the hands of police gave rise to worldwide crowds demanding an end to oppression and inequality.

In addition, the unprecedented foreign interference in our electoral process in both the 2016 and 2020 presidential elections resulted in highly politicized conversations around our electoral process.

The inept response to these changes was exacerbated by elected leaders lacking experience in crisis management and legislative process.

These situations have forced us to face the meaning of change in our lives. Change is constant. It is not just a contemporary phenomenon, though it appears that way given the readily accessible 24/7 news coverage. Viewing change from a historical perspective, I do believe that the study of history is really the study of change over time.

We have seen historic changes in the evolving role of women in our society, air travel spanning from the Wright Brothers to jumbo jets, and from the invention of Alexander Graham Bell's telephone to our cell phones. Change *is* constant and it raises the question of *How do we ride this escalating turbulent tide of change?*

Resilience as Constant as Change

If we can accept the constancy of change, we can also be comforted in knowing that the elements of resilience presented in this book are equally as constant and always available to us. Actively participating in, and contributing to, a world that is changing with breathtaking speed is not for the faint of heart.

And yet, the resiliency elements of **C**andor, **H**eroism, **A**cceptance, **N**urture, **G**ratitude, and **E**ngagement when integrated into our lives, result in ample opportunities for creativity, reinvention, and social problem solving.

As we enhance our resilience, we feel less overwhelmed by these immense changes. Our challenge is making the six resilience elements a habit, at a time when the demands in our lives and the world force us to be more outwardly focused.

I have witnessed how these elements have assisted others in leading more proactive lives, whether at home or at work.

A coaching client of mine clearly demonstrated his understanding of *nurture* when he called, expressing despair over his current situation. During our conversation, he recognized that when he engaged in nurturing activities, like physical exercise or treating himself to a massage, he was able to more proactively and creatively tackle the challenges of his situation. He knew that, regardless of what was occurring in his life, he must make these nurturing activities a priority.

A friend learned that practicing *candor* by being radically self-honest, she was able to face and accept that her long-term relationship was unhealthy. Embracing both the concepts of candor and heroism resulted in her ending the relationship, thereby achieving a sense of inner peace she hadn't experienced in a long time and creating a more satisfying life for herself.

In previous chapters, I told the stories of organizational leaders who, after acting on these six elements, were able to move their organizations forward in positive ways. To me, the evidence is clear. Incorporating and consistently practicing these elements does lead to greater feelings of personal control, whether at work or at home, in a world exhibiting what appears to be chaos.

A SUMMARY AND CALL TO ACTION

I believe the stories and examples here and throughout this book demonstrate that developing resiliency is both a mindset and a lifelong journey. Think of resilience as a mental and emotional muscle that needs exercising.

Some might think resilience is like a spring. If you stretch it and then let it go, it will return to its original form. This analogy works for me up to a point.

A spring does not possess the capacity to remember. I believe that when we are tested by an event or relationship, we learn important lessons as we move forward through the challenging situation. We then store our new wisdom in what I call our "resilience muscle."

I am pleased to discover that there is research that explains the dynamics behind the resilience muscle.

An expert in cognitive science, Dr. Pascale Michelon explains that our brains have a high degree of plasticity and, thus, have the ability to change throughout life.[47]

Elaborating on the plasticity concept, Dr. Norman Droidge, author of *The Brain that Changes Itself*, claims that the brain does not decline with age as science originally thought. He demonstrates that our brains retain the power to change and grow throughout life. Continually learning is what stimulates this brain growth.[48] From this research, we now know that resiliency muscles are real!

With every change challenge we confront, we stretch that resilience muscle. We store what we learned from the experience to help us move through the next change more easily. This process is how we accrue what I call "resilience wisdom." With every piece of this wisdom we gather along the way, we create a positive path forward for ourselves when it comes to responding to change.

My hope is that reading this book has launched you on your journey of developing your resilience wisdom. Just as we need nutrients to build body muscle, we need the six resiliency elements you have learned here to build your resilience muscle.

When faced with a given change, and you are truly honest with yourself about the impact of that change, and you communicate to others with *candor* what you are experiencing, you begin to conquer the fear you may be feeling about the change.

Your form of *heroism* emerges as you express your truth. While putting yourself "out there" may feel risky, it does lead you to taking positive action because you are grounded in what is true for you. Knowing this truth and acting on it helps you avoid becoming a victim of your situation.

Acceptance of a change, whether or not you agree with it, is made easier by assessing your own level of Emotional Intelligence. This knowledge allows you to observe your reaction to change rather than acting on your initial emotions.

Understanding EI results in emotional self-regulation. That allows you to state your feelings and avoid being emotionally hijacked by your brain's amygdala.

Your resilience muscle is further strengthened when you take the time to *nurture* yourself. The restorative properties of nurturing activities cannot be overstated.

The antidote to the stress of change is easily accessible. Be still. Go for a walk. Disconnect from technology. Practice mindfulness. Identify those activities that bring you calm and joy. Making them part of your daily life will keep you grounded during times of change!

The practice of expressing *gratitude* allows us to continuously view the glass of life as half full rather than half empty. No matter what the circumstance, I encourage you to find and focus on the good.

When devastating wildfires engulfed my state, literally wiping small towns off the map, I was heartened by the gratitude expressed by many of the survivors. They showed their gratitude for the many firefighters who risked their own lives to save theirs. Most importantly, the survivors expressed gratitude for what they did have rather than focusing on what they had lost.

Maintaining this attitude of gratitude provided the foundation for moving forward with their rebuilding efforts.

In addition to gratitude, the fire survivors demonstrated high *engagement* by pulling the threads of their shredded communities together, learning very quickly that community is about people—not the buildings and things.

When a change event occurs, you may find yourself withdrawing from the situation, which is a natural form of self-protection. It is at this point that staying engaged is crucial. Even more important is surrounding yourself with those who have a positive outlook on life. Hearing from those who are pessimistic about the situation can put you in a victim's state of mind very quickly.

As with the nature of change itself, resiliency is fluid and helps us maintain flexibility. I find a resilience activity in one instance may not be as effective the next time.

For example, the catastrophic wildfires in my state put my resiliency to the test. An avid hiker and walker, I watched with extreme sadness as many of my prize hiking areas were destroyed by fire. Normally, I would resolve such sadness by going for a long walk in my neighborhood's urban forest. Doing so was not possible. The smoke from the fires made the air quality near my home the worst in the world for at least six days and forced me to be house bound for that period.

Seeking other ways to deal with my sadness, I listened to uplifting music, read inspiring books, and increased my phone call outreach to friends. As a result, I was able to move through my sadness without being stuck in it.

A Call to Action

As we experienced with the COVID pandemic. we now recognize that thriving in a time of rapid and, often, cataclysmic change is the challenge of our time. This situation is likely to be customary, going forward. We have shifted, undeniably into a time of accelerated growth and change. If we can overcome our fear, we open up to creativity, wonderment, and new answers to propel us safely into the future. This experience can be ours when we accept that change is as natural as life itself—that life *is* about change.

Accumulating resiliency wisdom through the exercising of our resiliency muscle is now an important part of this life's journey—a journey *you* can start now!

Perhaps you don't know where to begin? Remember the words of C.S. Lewis "start where you are." The first question to ask yourself is *How are these six resilience elements showing up in my life right now?*

Your self-awareness is heightened once you explore your life through this new resiliency lens. With this awareness, you can break though this inner battle between resistance and resilience by gifting yourself these six elements. If, for example, you experience anxiety, instead of surrendering to panic, you are able choose acceptance. Acceptance can be made easier when you speak with candor to a colleague or a family member, nurture yourself with a long walk and expressing gratitude for all that is right in that moment.

You are not alone on this journey. It is a shared human experience that begs for us to be more engaged with one another. *Engagement* builds community and it is through community that our resilience is strengthened.

What would your life be like if you integrated these six elements into your daily life?

We no longer need to be paralyzed by change! Imagine how large your contributions to the world could be when you follow and consistently practice **C**andor, **H**eroism, **A**cceptance, **N**urture, **G**ratitude, and **E**ngagement! If we embrace these six elements, which will allow us to step into our best selves, we will, indeed, create a world that works for everyone.

And so, we have come to the end of our river journey. My hope is that from now on, as your life presents you with the roiling waters of change, you will experience yourself more like a river. You will be able to respond with an enhanced ability to flex and adapt!

Finally, I quote one of my favorite authors who said:

"You must live in the present,
launch yourself on every wave.
find your eternity in each and every moment."

HENRY DAVID THOREAU

ENDNOTES

1   M. K. Forbes and R. F. Krueger, "The Great Recession and Mental Health in the United States," *Clinical Psychological Science,* 7, no. 5 (July 2019): 900-913 https://tinyurl.com/yxhhustn

2   C. Margerison-Zilko, S. Goldman-Mellor, A. Falconi et.al., "Health Impacts of the Great Recession: A Critical Review," *Social Epidemiology,* 3 (February 3, 2016): 81-91 https://link.springer.com/article/10.1007/s40471-016-0068-6

3   CNN, April 16, 2020: https://tinyurl.com/yb9guu4p

4   CNN, April 5, 2020: https://tinyurl.com/sf7faul

5   D. Hamilton, "Calming Your Brain During Conflict," *Harvard Business Review* (December 22, 2015): https://tinyurl.com/zwpykx5

6   J. Kunnanatt, "Emotional Intelligence: The New Science of Interpersonal Effectiveness," *Human Resource Development Quarterly,* 15, no. 4 (December 8, 2004): 489-495, https://doi.org/10.1002/hrdq.1117

7   T. Creasey and J. Hiatt, Eds., *Best Practices in Change*

Management: 2012 Edition, Prosci Benchmarking Report (Loveland, CO: Prosci, 2012): www.change-management.com

8   M. C. Crowley, "Gallup's Workplace Jedi on How to Fix Our Employee Engagement Problem," *Fast Company* (June 14, 2013): https://tinyurl.com/y2ppmtx9

9   S. Scott, *Fierce Conversations: Achieving Success at Work & in Life, One Conversation at a Time* (New York, NY: New American Library, 2017): 1-349.

10   S. Stebbins, "The Influence of Community Service Volunteer Work on Perceptions of Job Satisfaction and Organizational Commitment among Oregon Employees of Pacific Northwest Bell," Unpublished Doctoral Dissertation, Oregon State University, Corvallis, Oregon, 1989. 26-27.

11   Z. E. Franco et al., "Heroism Research: A Review of Theories, Methods, Challenges and Trends," *Journal of Humanistic Psychology*, 58, no. 4 (December 21, 2016): 382-383.

12   E. L. Worthington, *Humility: The Quiet Virtue* (West Conshohoken, PA: Templeton Foundation Press, 2007): 45-46.

13   Z. Franco et. al.,5.

14   C. Pearson, *The Hero Within* (New York, NY: Harper/Elixir, 1986): 10-15.

15   E. Kinsella, T. Ritchie, and E. Igou, "Zeroing in on

Heroes: A Prototype Analysis of Hero Features," *Journal of Personality and Social Psychology,* 108, no. 1 (January 2015): 114–127.

16   C. Opfer, "Does Your Body Really Replace Itself Every Seven Years?": https://tinyurl.com/yctrx8zd

17   P. Chödrön, *The Places That Scare You* (Boulder, CO: Shambala Press, 2002): 21.

18   R. Heifetz, in Z. Herrmann, "The Challenge of Change," *Harvard Graduate School of Education Newsletter* (January 2017): https://www.gse.harvard.edu/uk/blog/challenge-change

19   A. Morin, "5 Signs and Symptoms of Empty Nest Syndrome" (2019): https://tinyurl.com/y2vtm8rp

20   W. Bridges, *Transitions: Making Sense of Life's Changes* (Philadelphia, PA: DeCapo Press, 2004): 45–47.

21   C. D. Scott and D. T. Jaffe, *Managing Organizational Change: A Practical Guide for Managers* (Menlo Park, CA: Crisp Publications, 1989): 35–46.

22   D. Goleman, *Emotional Intelligence: Why It Can Matter More than IQ* (New York: Random House, 2012): 15–25.

23   H. Gardner, in K. Cherry, "Is IQ or EQ More Important?" (December 6, 2019): https://tinyurl.com/y8zjc4y

24   J. Helliwell et al., *World Happiness Report 2019*, (New York: Sustainable Development Solutions Network, 2019): 128-133.

25   R. Holiday, *Stillness Is the Key* (New York, NY: Portfolio/ Penguin, 2019): 1-8.

26   M. Kalia, "Assessing the Economic Impact of Stress: The Modern Day Hidden Epidemic," *Metabolism*, 51, no. 6, suppl. 1 (June 2002): 49–53.

27   S. G. Aldana, in J. Grawitch et al., "The Path to a Healthy Workplace: A Critical Review Linking Healthy Workplace Practices, Employee Well-Being and Organizational Improvements," *Consulting Psychology Journal: Practice and Research*, 58, no. 3 (2006): 129–147.

28   J. Busbin and D. Campbell, "Employee Wellness Programs: A Strategy for Increasing Participation," *Journal of Health Care Marketing*, 10, no. 4 (December 1990): 22.

29   Holiday, p. 60.

30   A. Mathur, "2013 Best Year Yet for Alaska Tanker Company," *Occupational Health and Safety* (January 6, 2014): https://ohsonline.com/articles/2014/01/06/2013-best-year-yet-for-alaska-tanker-company.aspx

31   J. Greeson, "Mindfulness Research Update: 2008," *Complementary Health Practice Review*, 14, no. 1 (January 2009): 10–18.

32   W. Muller, *Sabbath: Finding Renewal and Delight in Our Daily Lives* (New York, NY: Bantam Publishing, 2000): 35–40.

33   Q. Li, "'Forest Bathing' Is Good for Your Health. Here's How to Do It," *Time* (May 1, 2018): https://time.com/5259602/japanese-forest-bathing/

34   R. Sansone and L. Sansone, "Gratitude and Well Being: The Benefits of Appreciation," *Psychiatry*, 7, no. 11 (2010): 18–22.

35   A. Wood et al., "The Role of Gratitude in the Development of Social Support, Stress and Depression: Two Longitudinal Studies," *Journal of Research in Personality*, 42 (2008): 847.

36   R. Emmons, *Thanks: How the New Science of Gratitude Can Make You Happier* (New York, NY: Houghton-Mifflin, 2007), 35.

37   Wood et al., 848.

38   K. Kruse, *Employee Engagement for Everyone: 4 Keys to Happiness and Fulfillment at Work* (Philadelphia, PA: The Center for Wholehearted Leadership, 2013): 6.

39   J. Harter, "Employee Engagement on the Rise in the U.S.," *Gallup* (August 26, 2018): https://news.gallup.com/poll/241649/employee-engagement-rise.aspx

40   Harter.

41   C. Swarnalatha and T. S. Prasanna, "Employee

Engagement and Change Management," *International Journal of Business and Management Invention,* 2, no. 61 (June 2013): 1–6.

42   D. Baer, "Milwaukee Shows what Segregation Does to Cities," The Cut, *New York* (2014): https://www.thecut. com/2016/08/milwaukee-shows-what-segregation-does-to-american-cities.html

43   C. Caref et. al., "The Black and White of Education in Chicago's Public Schools," *Chicago Teachers Union* (November 30, 2012): https://www.ctulocal1.org/ wp-content/uploads/2018/10/CTU-black-and-white-of-chicago-education.pdf

44   N. Eberstadt, "The 'New Normal': Thoughts about the Shape of Things to Come in the Post-Pandemic World," *The National Bureau of Asian Research* (April 18, 2020): https://www.nbr.org/publication/the-new-normal-thoughts-about-the-shape-of-things-to-come-in-the-post-pandemic-world/

45   Z. Abbany, "What Do Futurists Imagine for the Post-Corona-Virus Pandemic?" *Deutsche Welle* (February 4, 2020): https://www.dw.com/en/what-do-futurists-imagine-for-the-post-coronavirus-pandemic-world/a-52993740

46   A. Leaf, "Potential Health Effects of Global Climatic and Environmental Changes," *The New England Journal of Medicine* (December 7, 1989): https://www. nejm.org/doi/full/10.1056/NEJM198912073212305

47   P. Michelon, "Brain Plasticity: How Learning Changes
      Your Brain," Sharp Brains (February 26, 2008): https://
      sharpbrains.com/blog/2008/02/26/brain-plasticity-how-
      learning-changes-your-brain/

48   N. Droidge, *The Brain That Changes Itself: Stories of
      Personal Triumph from the Frontiers of Brain Science*
      (New York, NY: Penguin Books; 2007).

WORKS CITED

Abbany, Z. "What Do Futurists Imagine for the Post-Corona-Virus Pandemic?" *Deutsche Welle* (February 4, 2020): https://www.dw.com/en/what-do-futurists-imagine-for-the-post-coronavirus-pandemic-world/a-52993740

Baer, D. "Milwaukee Shows what Segregation Does to Cities." The Cut, New York (2014):, https://www.thecut.com/2016/08/milwaukee-shows-what-segregation-does-to-american-cities.htm

Bridges, W. *Transitions: Making Sense of Life's Changes.* Philadelphia, PA: DeCapo Press, 2004Busbin, J., and D. Campbell. "Employee Wellness Programs: A Strategy for Increasing Participation." *Journal of Health Care Marketing,* 10, no. 4 (December 1990): 22

Caref, C., S. Hainds, K. Hilgendorf, P. Jankof, and K. Russell. "The Black and White of Education in Chicago's Public Schools." *Chicago Teachers Union* (November 30, 2012): https://www.ctulocal1.org/wp-content/uploads/2018/10/CTU-black-and-white-of-chicago-education.pd

Cherry, K. "Is IQ or EQ More Important?" (December 6, 2019): https://tinyurl.com/y8zjc4yt

Chödrön, P. *The Places That Scare You.* Boulder, CO: Shambala Press, 2002CNN, April 5, 2020, https://tinyurl.com/sf7faul

CNN, April 16, 2020, https://tinyurl.com/yb9guu4p

Creasey, T., and J. Hiatt (eds.). *Best Practices in Change Management: 2012 Edition,* Prosci Benchmarking Report. Loveland, CO: Prosci, 2012

Crowley, M. C. "Gallup's Workplace Jedi on How to Fix Our Employee Engagement Problem." *Fast Company* (June 14, 2013), https://tinyurl.com/y2ppmtx9

Droidge, N. *The Brain That Changes Itself: Stories of Personal Triumph from the Frontiers of Brain Science.* New York, NY: Penguin Books, 2007

Eberstadt, N. "The 'New Normal': Thoughts about the Shape of Things to Come in the Post-Pandemic World." *The National Bureau of Asian Research* (April 18, 2020): https://www.nbr.org/publication/the-new-normal-thoughts-about-the-shape-of-things-to-come-in-the-post-pandemic-world/

Forbes, M. K., and R. F. Krueger. "The Great Recession and Mental Health in the United States." *Clinical Psychological Science,* 7, no. 5 (July 2019): 900-913, https://tinyurl.com/yxhhustn

Franco, Z. E., S. T. Allison, E. L. Kinsella, A. Kohen, M. Langdon, and P. G. Zimbardo. "Heroism Research: A Review of Theories, Methods, Challenges and Trends," *Journal of Humanistic Psychology,* 58, no. 4 (December 21, 2016), 1–19

Goleman, D. *Emotional Intelligence: Why It Can Matter More than IQ*. New York: Random House, 2012

Grawitch, J., M. Gottschalk, and D. Munz, "The Path to a Healthy Workplace: A Critical Review Linking Healthy Workplace Practices, Employee Well-Being and Organizational Improvements." Consulting Psychology Journal: Practice and Research, 58, no. 3 (2006): 129–147

Greeson, J. "Mindfulness Research Update: 2008." *Complementary Health Practice Review,* 14, no. 1 (January 2009): 10–18

Hamilton, D. "Calming Your Brain During Conflict." *Harvard Business Review* (December 22, 2015), https:// tinyurl.com/zwpykx5

Harter, J. "Employee Engagement on the Rise in the U.S." *Gallup* (August 26, 2018): https://news.gallup.com/ poll/241649/employee-engagement-rise.aspx

Helliwell, J., R. Layard, and J. Sachs. *World Happiness Report 2019*. New York: Sustainable Development Solutions Network, 2019

Herrmann, Z. "The Challenge of Change." *Harvard Graduate School of Education Newsletter* (January 2017), https://www.gse.harvard.edu/uk/blog/challenge-change

Holiday, R. *Stillness Is the Key.* New York, NY: Portfolio/ Penguin, 2019

Kalia, M. "Assessing the Economic Impact of Stress: The Modern Day Hidden Epidemic." *Metabolism,* 51, no. 6, suppl. 1 (June 2002): 49–53

Kinsella, E., T. Ritchie, and E. Igou. "Zeroing in on Heroes: A Prototype Analysis of Hero Features." *Journal of Personality and Social Psychology,* 108, no. 1 (January 2015), pp. 114–127

Kruse, K. *Employee Engagement for Everyone: 4 Keys to Happiness and Fulfillment at Work.* Philadelphia, PA: The Center for Wholehearted Leadership, 2013

Kunnanatt, J. "Emotional Intelligence: The New Science of Interpersonal Effectiveness." *Human Resource Development Quarterly,* 15, no. 4 (December 8, 2004):489-495

Leaf, A. "Potential Health Effects of Global Climatic and Environmental Changes." *The New England Journal of Medicine* (December 7, 1989): https://www.nejm.org/doi/full/10.1056/NEJM198912073212305

Li, Q. "'Forest Bathing' Is Good for Your Health. Here's How to Do It." *Time* (May 1, 2018): https://time.com/5259602/japanese-forest-bathing/

Margerison-Zilko, C., S. Goldman-Mellor, A. Falconi et al. "Health Impacts of the Great Recession: A Critical Review. Social Epidemiology, 3 (February 3, 2016): https://tinyurl.com/yxpearw4

Mathur, A. "2013 Best Year Yet for Alaska Tanker Company." *Occupational Health and Safety* (January 6, 2014): https://

ohsonline.com/articles/2014/01/06/2013-best-year-yet-for-alaska-tanker-company.aspx

Michelon, P. "Brain Plasticity: How Learning Changes Your Brain." *Sharp Brains* (February 26, 2008): https://sharpbrains.com/blog/2008/02/26/brain-plasticity-how-learning-changes-your-brain/

Morin, A. "5 Signs and Symptoms of Empty Nest Syndrome" (2019), https://tinyurl.com/y2vtm8rp

Muller, W. *Sabbath: Finding Renewal and Delight in Our Daily Lives.* New York, NY: Bantam Publishing, 2000

Opfer, C. "Does Your Body Really Replace Itself Every Seven Years?" https://tinyurl.com/yctrx8zd

Pearson, C. *The Hero Within.* New York, NY: Harper/Elixer, 1986

Sansone, R., and L. Sansone. "Gratitude and Well Being: The Benefits of Appreciation." *Psychiatry*, 7, no. 11 (2010): 18–22

Scott, C. D., and D. T. Jaffe. *Managing Organizational Change: A Practical Guide for Managers.* Menlo Park, CA: Crisp Publications, 1989

Scott, S. *Fierce Conversations: Achieving Success at Work & in Life, One Conversation at a Time.* New York, NY: New American Library, 2017

Stebbins, S. "The Influence of Community Service Volunteer Work on Perceptions of Job Satisfaction and Organizational Commitment among Oregon Employees of Pacific Northwest Bell," Unpublished Doctoral Dissertation, Oregon State University, Corvallis, Oregon, 1989

Swarnalatha, C., and T. S. Prasanna. "Employee Engagement and Change Management." *International Journal of Business and Management Invention,* 2, no. 61 (June 2013): 1–6

Wood, A., J. Matlby, R. Gillett, P. Linley, and S. Joseph, "The Role of Gratitude in the Development of Social Support, Stress and Depression: Two Longitudinal Studies," *Journal of Research in Personality,* 42 (2008): 854–871

Worthington, E. L. Humility: *The Quiet Virtue.* West Conshohoken, PA: Templeton Foundation Press, 2007

ADDITIONAL RESOURCES

Coetzee M., and N. Harry. "Emotional Intelligence as a Predictor of Employees' Career Adaptability." *Journal of Vocational Behavior*, 84, no. 1 (February 2014): 90–97.

Cook, S. M.-K. "Managing the Inevitability of Change." *RN Journal* (2019): https://rn-journal.com/journal-of-nursing/managing-the-inevitability-of-change.

Csikszentmihalyi, M. *Finding Flow*. New York, NY: Basic Books, 1997.

Emmons, R.: *Thanks: How the New Science of Gratitude Can Make You Happier*. New York, NY: Houghton-Mifflin, 2007.

Hunter, J. "Why Mindfulness Matters." *Claremont Graduate University* (July 29, 2014): https://www.cgu.edu/news/2014/07/jeremy-hunter/.

Jones, K. B. "The Dangers of the Empty Nest Syndrome." *U Health, University of Utah* (October 7, 2014): https://healthcare.utah.edu/the-scope/shows.php?shows=0_etom70c6.

Kohll, A. "The Evolving Definition of Work-Life Balance." *Forbes* (March 2018): https://www.forbes.com/sites/alankohll/2018/03/27/the-evolving-definition-of-work-life-balance/#30a93de19ed3.

Livni, E. "The Japanese Practice of 'Forest Bathing' Is Scientifically Proven to Improve Your Health." Quartz (October 12, 2016): https://qz.com/804022/health-benefits-japanese-forest-bathing/.

Mancini, J., and K. Roberto. *Pathways of Human Development: Explorations of Change.* New York, NY: Lexington Books, 2009.

Quinn, R. *Deep Change: Discovering the Leader Within.* San Francisco, CA: Jossey-Bass, 1996.

INDEX

ABOUT THE AUTHOR

Sarah Stebbins is adjunct faculty at Portland State University, Portland Oregon where she pursues her 25+ year consulting career. A successful Change Management Consultant and Certified Professional Coach, Dr. Stebbins works with diverse organizations locally and nationally. Her vision is to transform organizations into "healthy working communities, one employee at a time." More information about Dr. Stebbins and her work can be found at www.thebetterchange.com.